The Fugitive Slave Law and Anthony Burns: A Problem in Law Enforcement

Jane H. Pease

William H. Pease
University of Maine

The America's Alternatives Series
Edited by **Harold M. Hyman**

The Fugitive Slave Law and Anthony Burns:

A Problem in Law Enforcement

J. B. Lippincott Company
Philadelphia/New York/Toronto

ISBN 0-397-47329-X
Library of Congress Catalog Card Number 74-23063
Printed in the United States of America

1 3 5 7 9 8 6 4 2

Library of Congress Cataloging in Publication Data

Pease, Jane H.
  The fugitive slave law and Anthony Burns.

  (The America's alternatives series)
  Bibliography: p.
  1. Fugitive slave law of 1850. 2. Slavery in
the United States — Fugitive slaves. 3. Burns, Anthony,
1834-1862. I. Pease, William Henry, 1924-   joint
author. II. Title.
E450.P35   301.44'93'0973   74-23063
ISBN 0-397-47329-X

Contents

Foreword

"When you judge decisions, you have to judge them in the light of what there was available to do it," noted Secretary of State George C. Marshall to the Senate Committees on the Armed Services and Foreign Relations in May 1951.[1] In this spirit, each volume in the "America's Alternatives" series examines the past for insights which History—perhaps only History—is peculiarly fitted to offer. In each volume the author seeks to learn why decision-makers in crucial public policy or, more rarely, private choice situations adopted a course and rejected others. Within this context of choices, the author may ask what influence then-existing expert opinion, administrative structures, and budgetary factors exerted in shaping decisions? What weights did constitutions or traditions have? What did men hope for or fear? On what information did they base their decisions? Once a decision was made, how was the decision-maker able to enforce it? What attitudes prevailed toward nationality, race, region, religion, or sex, and how did these attitudes modify results?

We freely ask such questions of the events of our time. This "America's Alternatives" volume transfers appropriate versions of such queries to the past.

In examining those elements that were a part of a crucial historical decision, the author has refrained from making judgments based upon attitudes, information, or values that were not current at the time the decision was made. Instead, as much as possible he or she has explored the past in terms of data and prejudices known to persons contemporary to the event.

1. U.S. Senate, Hearings Before the Committees on the Armed Services and the Foreign Relations of the United States, *The Military Situation in the Far East* (82 Cong., 2d sess.), Part I, p. 382. Professor Ernest R. May's "Alternatives" volume directed me to this source and quotation.

Nevertheless, the following reconstruction of one of America's major alternative choices speaks implicitly and frequently, explicitly to present concerns.

In form, this volume consists of a narrative and analytical historical essay (Part One), within which the author has identified by use of headnotes (i.e., Alternative A, etc.) the choices which he believes were actually before the decision-makers with whom he is concerned.

Part Two of this volume contains, in whole or part, the most appropriate source documents that illustrate the Part One Alternatives. The Part Two Documents and Part One essay are keyed for convenient use (i.e., references in Part One will direct readers to appropriate Part Two Documents). The volume's Part Three offers users further guidance in the form of a Bibliographic Essay.

Abraham Lincoln's generation grew to maturity with only two seemingly insoluble public-policy questions to mar its all-conquering pattern. Both these wearying, undying matters centered on the presence of large numbers of black people in white America, black people whose legal status was defined by states and localities except in the federal District and in the national territories. The only time that the national authority entered states in situations involving American blacks, was to return runaway Negroes to owners in other states. In short, the slave-property interest of a slave state was able to employ the national authority as a bridge across the federal system and to penetrate states where slave property could not exist. But the traffic was one-way only; free state law codes could not employ the national authority and demand remedies in slave states.

Thus the runaway Negro became the symbol of a federalism which many Northerners felt was skewed in favor of the slave states. Professors Jane and William Pease present here the story of one of the most dramatic fugitive slave incidents which reinforced both Northern fears that slavery eroded the rights of free men in their own section and white Southern fears that abolitionism increasingly threatened their section's property rights and personal security.

Harold M. Hyman
Rice University

Acknowledgments

The authors, as always, are indebted to numerous libraries for making materials available to them. They wish specifically to thank the following institutions and their staffs for assistance in preparing this book: the University of Florida Library, the Charleston Library Society, the Manuscripts Division of the Library of Congress, the National Archives, the Boston Public Library, the Massachusetts Historical Society, the Federal Records Center at Waltham, Massachusetts, the Houghton Library, the New Hampshire Historical Society, and the Fogler Library of the University of Maine.

For permission to quote from manuscripts in their charge, the authors wish to thank the Trustees of the Boston Public Library, the Harvard College Library, and the Massachusetts Historical Society. Finally, we must thank Betsey Miller Shaffer for her impeccable typing.

Part One

The Fugitive Slave Law and Anthony Burns

1

Passing the Law

Seldom since the United States became a nation has any law generated as much moral opposition as did the Fugitive Slave Law of 1850. Never have property rights and civil liberties clashed more starkly than when men and women in the free states were called on to return fugitive slaves to bondage. Nonetheless, the tensions they faced had long been building and had their roots in the very framing of the Constitution in 1787. By then several Northern states had already ended slavery within their own borders; yet the constitutional convention in its efforts to achieve a more strongly unified nation acted to insure the interests of slave holders. In doing so, the convention adopted a compromise which provided that each slave be counted as three fifths of a person for purposes of both taxation and congressional representation, and which forestalled ending the African slave trade for at least twenty years. Finally its members expressly wrote into the Constitution the provision that "No Person held to Service or Labour in one State, under the Laws thereof, escaping into another, shall, in Consequence of any Law or Regulation therein, be discharged from such Service or Labour, but shall be delivered up on Claim of the Party to whom such Service or Labour may be due" (Art. IV, Sec. II, Par. 3.). Both Northerners and Southerners believed that these were necessary provisions to balance sectional interests and soothe sectional fears.

In 1808, Congress ended the international slave trade and that issue was, thereafter, little debated. Never until post-Civil War Reconstruction was federal action taken to amend the three fifths ratio. But the third provision twice required national legislation and ultimately created far more sectional rancor than it allayed. That this would be the case was not initially clear. In 1793, Congress first provided for enforcing the return of fugitives from labor in an act designed primarily to insure extradition of fugitives from justice. The law required that federal, state, and local officials in any state to which a fugitive had escaped from another were responsible for his return once the owner or his agent had apprehended the runaway. That Congress anticipated some Northern opposition to the law was evident in the provision that any one who helped a slave escape or hid him from his master was subject to a $500 fine. Despite that provision, the law at first provoked little overt opposition and was regarded simply as a means to implement a binding constitutional obligation.

Limiting the 1793 Law

Before long, however, the finality implicit in that constitutional compromise began to crumble. Northerners, many of whom were troubled by slavery though they did not support black equality with whites, hesitated to return salves escaping into their states. While they might tolerate slavery as an institution elsewhere and recognize rights to property in slaves, they would not themselves act to deprive individual human beings of liberty. So, even before a broadly based antislavery movement had emerged, there was resistance to the law's enforcement. In Pennsylvania, which had long sustained a society for promoting the abolition of slavery and had early acted to end slavery within its own borders, the legislature passed laws in 1820 and 1826 to define and limit the state's role in enforcing the 1793 federal statute. Though these laws regularized the procedures by which claimants might recover their property, they also stipulated somewhat more adequate protection for alleged fugitives. They provided, for instance, that their cases would be heard by judges rather than by mere aldermen or justices of the peace and that certain standards of evidence would be maintained. They also levied severe penalties against the illegal seizure (kidnapping) of free blacks.

More persistent and overt opposition to the 1793 statute emerged with the antislavery movement's growth after 1830. Then local and state societies, as well as the American Anti-Slavery Society, founded in 1833, nourished a growing abolitionist sentiment. William Lloyd Garrison's *Liberator* and the national society's *Emancipator* were but parts of a flood of propaganda so alarming to Southerners that in 1836 the Charleston, South Carolina, postmaster confiscated abolitionist literature coming through the mails and with the help of his fellow townsmen burned it. In the North, fiery lecturers like evangelist Theodore Weld and British visitor George Thompson stirred audiences both to anger and conversion while Charleston-born Angelina Grimké and Philadelphia Quaker Lucretia Mott roused humanitarian sympathy for the slave. Even Washington felt the new mood. In 1836 abolitionists flooded the Congress with petitions protesting the possible annexation of Texas and seeking an end to slavery and the slave trade in the District of Columbia; petitions which, despite the efforts of ex-president John Quincy Adams, the House of Representatives tabled undebated.

With the increase of Northern antislavery sentiment came more pronounced sympathy for fugitive slaves. Although they were most often aided by blacks, white abolitionists also helped, giving legal and financial aid as well as shelter and sustenance. More formally, vigilance committees were organized to coordinate these efforts in cities to which runaways most frequently came. In addition, in individual cases, local Negroes used mob action to rescue fugitives from law officers, as they did in Detroit and Buffalo; and in Boston a group of angry black women spirited a refugee out of a court room in the very presence of the presiding judge. By 1840 it was clear that abolitionists were willing to use both legal and illegal means to protect the new-found liberty of human beings who had, in their flight north, rebelled against being mere chattel.

Necessarily these activities provoked serious clashes between the Southern determination to protect slave property and the increasing Northern proclivity to pit the human rights of the slave against the property rights of the master. Frequently the issue focussed on the responsibility of Northern state officials to facilitate enforcement of the 1793 law and on Southern moves to circumvent obstacles which increasingly blocked the return of runaways. In 1839 the governor of Virginia, impatient with the failure of the 1793 law to return slaves escaping from his state on Northern vessels, called upon New York governor William Seward to extradite three sailors "charged with having feloniously stolen a negro slave"[1] in Virginia. Arguing that, because slavery did not exist in New York, the state could recognize no such crime. Seward refused to extradite the sailors. Three years later, the federal Supreme Court moved to define more precisely the state's responsibility in fugitive slave law cases. Edward Prigg, a Maryland resident, had seized his fugitive slave and her children and removed them from Pennsylvania in clear violation of the legal processes required by that state's 1826 law. After a state court had tried and convicted Prigg, both Maryland, concerned with her citizens' property rights, and Pennsylvania, eager to protect her residents' civil liberties, backed Prigg's appeal to the Supreme Court. That tribunal deliberated two central points: first, whether the power to legislate under the fugitive slave provision of the Constitution resided with the nation or with the states; and second, whether federal law could oblige state officials to execute the federal fugitive slave law.

The decision, written by Justice Joseph Story, ruled that there was no constitutional requirement that state authorities must in any way assist in returning fugitive slaves, although state magistrates might, if they chose, "exercise that authority, unless prohibited by state legislation."[2] But except for that point, congressional legislation on the subject took precedence over all state legislation. The nimbleness of the Court's finding elicited mixed responses from both pro- and antislavery people—each side finding some merit and some fault with it. Nonetheless the decision marked a fundamental shift in Southern views of federal and state power. Many Southerners heretofore associated with a strict states' rights position, which prohibited federal interference with their peculiar institution, now pressed for an extension of federal power to protect their property rights. By contrast, antislavery Northerners demanded a strict observance of the states' power to guarantee to all their residents, including fugitives, the rights of habeas corpus* and trial by jury.

As a result of the Prigg decision, personal liberty laws similar to those of Pennsylvania proliferated in the Northeast. Even before 1842, both New York and Vermont had guaranteed fugitives the rights to jury trial and counsel. Thereafter, Massachusetts, responding specifically to the arrest of the fugitive George Latimer in Boston, prohibited the use of state jails for detaining fugitives as well as any participation by state officials in enforcing the fugitive slave law. Subsequently Pennsylvania, Rhode Island, and Vermont also forbade state officials, as one observer put it, to "act the part

---

*A common law writ whose object is to bring an arrested person speedily before a court or judge and thus prevent his or her illegal imprisonment.

of bull-dog for the South, to seize and hold their runaway slaves,"[3] or otherwise to assist in enforcing the law.

The Compromise of 1850

Over the years therefore Northern unwillingness to implement the constitutional provision for the return of fugitives from labor trenched on Southern demands for its strict enforcement and led to a fundamental constitutional issue. To the South, this guarantee of its property rights was part of a compromise which had led it to accept the Constitution in the first place. Antislavery Northerners, unwilling to be bound by a compromise they considered an infringement of human rights, argued a superior moral commitment or "higher law" which absolved them from complying with the obligations imposed by the Constitution. This disagreement over the binding nature of a fundamental national compromise festered in the congressional debates which followed the Mexican War. Confronted with newly acquired territory, where slavery's status required definition, Congress argued not only the federal government's power to establish or ban slavery but its responsibility to insure the return of fugitives.

In January 1850 Senator Henry Clay of Kentucky, venerated for his past role in mediating national crises, proposed one more national compromise whereby the United States might balance opposing sectional issues. In the process Southerners were asked to surrender a parity of free and slave states, which the admission of California as a free state involved, in return for equal access for slave owners to the rest of the Mexican cession and a new and binding fugitive slave law. In turn antislavery Yankees were to be pacified with abolition of the slave trade in the District of Columbia.

From the outset it was obvious that new fugitive slave legislation faced serious problems. The bill's first version, introduced by Chairman Andrew P. Butler of South Carolina for the Senate Judiciary Committee, had failed to spark Senate action in the two previous sessions in which it had been presented. The bill's clear purpose was to expand federal power in order to guarantee the return of fugitive slaves. Compensating for the Prigg decision's limiting those who must enforce the 1793 law, the new bill would authorize virtually all federal appointees from judges, clerks, and commissioners of the circuit and district courts to marshals, postmasters, and collectors of customs to issue certificates legalizing the rendition of fugitives from one state to another. In order to discourage slave rescues and to succor unsuccessful claimants, the bill proposed increasing the fine for obstructing the return of a fugitive from $500 to $1,000 and paying it to the claimant.

Within a week, however, Senator Butler had withdrawn the Judiciary Committee's bill in favor of a substitute offered by James Mason of Virginia. Similar to the original in spirit, the Mason version spelled out more explicitly the procedures to be followed in the territories as well as other details of enforcement. More important than any of these specifics was the fact that Mason presented a new bill rather than amending Butler's. That the South

Carolinian stepped aside in favor of the Virginian was significant in itself of the upper South's overriding practical concern for an effective fugitive slave law (Document I-A-1). In introducing the original bill, Butler had asserted that the estimated $200,000 annual loss from runaways concentrated almost wholly in the border states of Kentucky, Virginia, Maryland, and Missouri. Nonetheless the deep South had as profound an interest as the upper South in maintaining the guarantees of Southern interests embodied in the Constitution, and in upholding thereby the unalterable nature of the federal compromise of 1787. The importance of an effective fugitive slave law, although it served primarily the practical interests of the upper South, lay in its symbolic confirmation of the inviolability of the right of property in slaves throughout the South.

But to have symbolic meaning, the law must be effective, and throughout the debate on the new fugitive slave law Mason and Butler constantly addressed the question of enforceability. The constitutional provision for the return of fugitives from labor, as they understood it, imposed obligations on the individual states to enforce it. Consequently, although ultimate legislative power belonged to the federal Congress, as Senator Butler pointed out, "it was and is the duty of the States themselves to provide by positive legislation for the same object."[4]

Nothing less, the South thought, fulfilled the spirit of the original constitutional compromise, for which the South had paid in allowing Congress the power to pass commercial and navigation legislation beneficial to the North. Now the South saw the North, rich and prosperous as a result of this compromise, unwilling to abide by its obligations to protect slave property. There was a time, Mason nostalgically recalled, when the states behaved toward each other in sisterly fashion. But that spirit had died, he observed sadly, wondering the while whether any law could revive it.

Dispite Mason's nostalgia, virtually no senator believed that Northern public opinion, which had so long drawn back from its constitutional obligations, would change. Those who had passed personal liberty laws and had otherwise thwarted the enforcement of the 1793 law were unlikely to change their minds in the face of stiffer legislation. "I know this much," Senator Butler observed when he first introduced his bill, "that the cardinal articles of the Constitution are not to be preserved by statutory enactments upon parchment. They must live and be preserved in the willing minds and good faith of those who incurred the obligation to maintain them."[5] Senator Mason added resignedly, "I have but little hope that it [a new fugitive slave law] will afford the remedy it is intended to afford."[6] Seven months later, during the final debate on the bill, the situation was unchanged. Replying to a proposal to designate one federal commissioner per county who would be charged with the return of fugitives, the Virginia senator contended that "you could not get these commissioners to execute the law, because if they did they would incur the odium of all their neighbors, and be themselves put under the ban."[7] Jefferson Davis of Mississippi seconded these dour observations. Though he was willing to support a new fugitive law, he nevertheless assured his colleagues that he "never considered it a matter of very much importance" because, unless the North made some effort to return fugitives as the Constitution required, he doubted "the efficacy of any law that [might] be passed by Congress on the subject."[8] As he had predicted months earlier, the new law would remain "a dead letter" wherever public opinion refused it countenance.[9]

Many Northerners agreed heartily with Davis's conclusions. William Seward, former New York governor and now a senator, distilled much Northern sentiment in his "higher law" speech. Although speaking primarily on the question of the admission of California, Seward also discussed the Fugitive Slave Law of 1793. Its inefficacy, he argued, did not result from the "leniency of its provisions" but rather from its denial of civil rights to alleged fugitives and its consequent affront to public opinion. "Has any Government," he asked his colleagues, "ever succeeded in changing the moral convictions of its subjects by force?"[10] Seward had, in fact, proposed an alternate fugitive slave bill to Mason's, more consistent with his section's concept of the higher law because it granted alleged fugitives habeas corpus and trial by jury (Document I-B-1). Yet his proposal had been disingenuous, for its other provisions, in passing on the financial costs of legal action to the claimant, would have deterred almost all masters from taking action to reclaim escaped slaves. Adopting Seward's general position, John P. Hale, Free Soiler of New Hampshire, continued, during the debate on Mason's bill, to champion just such guarantees as the New Yorker's substitute had included. When Senator Pratt of Maryland objected, Hale replied that even in the slave states, slaves claiming to be free were entitled to a trial to establish the fact. And, in a final twist, Hale noted that the Mason bill nowhere restricted the summary process to blacks and that it consequently threatened the civil rights of every American.

The position which Seward and Hale had taken was not, as their critics charged, a maverick extreme, but represented a widely shared Northern point of view. Daniel Webster, who in his March 7 speech angered many Northerners by supporting the entire Clay compromise, offered, in early June, a substitute fugitive slave bill which guaranteed trial by jury to alleged fugitives claiming to be free. Two months later, after Webster had left the Senate to join President Fillmore's cabinet, Senator William Dayton of New Jersey reintroduced Webster's substitute even though he shared his constituents' view that fugitives were a "pest and an annoyance"[11] who should be returned according to law. And despite the Southern business connections of his political backers, Webster's replacement, Cotton Whig Robert Winthrop of Boston, supported Dayton, cautioning the Senate that "if there be a strong sense of the injustice and oppressiveness of any particular provision, whether of this law or of any other, there will alway[s] be more or less of opposition to its execution"[12] (Document I-C-1). What was absolutely clear—and no alert Southerner could have missed it—was that many of the Northerners who supported a stronger fugitive slave law considered guarantees of due process essential to its enforcement. Among their constituents, a concern for civil liberties overshadowed maintaining the absolute property rights of slave owners. Deny that concern and the fugitive slave law would encounter significant opposition.

The puzzle facing Congress, therefore, was how to protect Southern slave interests and, simultaneously, satisfy Northern civil liberties demands. Was it possible to satisfy both claims and avoid the clash between property rights and human freedom? Some, at least, saw a way out by a system of financial compensation. Maryland Senator Thomas Pratt, reflecting his state's practical interest in a solution of the problem, proposed that the federal government pay the claimant the value of any runaway slave who was located by his owner in another state but for some reason was not then returned (Document I-D-1). The constitutional compromise, the law of 1793, and the Prigg decision, Pratt insisted, all asserted the federal government's responsibility to insure the return of fugitives from labor. It followed logically from that premise that if government could not fulfill its obligations it should make good its failure by compensating the owner for his loss.

Pratt's proposal, offered late in August 1850, attracted some support but failed to satisfy objections made to it from both North and South. Senator Dayton of New Jersey opposed it because he feared it would drain the federal treasury. The rationale behind Pratt's proposal could be extended to hold the federal government responsible, at unimaginable cost to the taxpayers, for all damages incurred when any federal law was broken. Butler of South Carolina took up where Dayton left off, predicting that should the Pratt proposal prevail, the federal government would become one vast underwriter, repairing "all the losses which individuals or States may sustain, because another State fails to perform its Constitutional obligation."[13] And that, even were the compensation limited to the fugitive slave obligation, would lead to fraud, for who would genuinely try to recover property when he could so easily claim compensation (Document I-D-2). Thus North and deep South rejected this border state proposal.

Interestingly, at least one antislavery senator saw in the compensation idea a means for federal action toward emancipation within the slave states. Early in 1851 Senator Seward privately queried a political friend in New York for his reaction to a federal law which would permit a fugitive to retain his freedom upon paying his owner the value assessed by a court in the owner's home state. Seward never made his proposal public, but had he done so he would only have reinforced Southern opposition to federal action on compensation. Jefferson Davis of Mississippi had foreseen the danger that compensation would prove an opening wedge and opposed Pratt's proposal for extending federal power to interfere with slavery in the states. Thus even had a potential drain on public monies not been a deterrent to the Pratt amendment, it would have received little support.

When monetary compensation proved an unacceptable means to reconcile North and South, the racial prejudice they both shared presented the best protection for slave owners' rights. Seward had noted this potential in his speech on the admission of California when he observed that "slavery has a guaranty ... in the prejudices of caste and color, which induce even large majorities in all the free States to regard sympathy with the slave as an act of unmanly humiliation and self-abasement."[14] Jefferson Davis turned that very situation against the Pratt amendment arguing that once the door to the treasury was opened, Congress might provide funds to ship free Negroes to Africa. If the North were thus relieved "from the best check we have upon the popular feeling in favor of runaway slaves," Northern "unwillingness to have negroes among them," the South would lose the only "practical, wholesome restraint upon the growing disposition to violate our property right."[15] The following year, when Seward was pondering his compensation scheme, Senator Jeremiah Clemens of Alabama pursued Davis's point, claiming that the South was best protected by the laws of various middle western states which absolutely prohibited all Negro in-migration. Clemens praised these states for doing "precisely what we wanted done—they have struck at the root of the evil." Not only did they permit Southerners to enforce the fugitive slave law, they almost made the law superfluous, saying that "fugitives shall not come among them."[16]

Such legislation, however, was an unlikely solution in those states most disposed to defy the fugitive statute, for there the exercise of states' rights was turned to defiance rather than enforcement. Congressman Joshua Giddings, Ohio Free Soiler from the antislavery Western Reserve, argued against federal intervention in slave matters no less fervently than did Senator Davis of Mississippi. The federal government, he told his colleagues in December 1850, "possesses no more right to involve the people of the North in the support of southern slavery, than it has to involve us in the support of Russian serfdom. Congress possesses no more power nor right to make us the catchers of southern slaves, than of Russian serfs."[17] Four months later, Seward damned the fugitive slave law as "an attempt by a purely federative government to extend the economy of slave States"[18] into the free states. And in 1852, arguing constitutional principles similar to those of his Whig colleague, Robert Rantoul, Jr., the Democratic senator from Massachusetts stressed that the law illegitimately assigned power to the federal government which was reserved under the Constitution to the states.

What options, then, were open to the South in her efforts to protect slave property? Compensation held at least the potential for subsequent federal intervention to effect emancipation. Reliance on Northern prejudice to produce state legislation excluding all Negro migrants simply did not work in the Northeast. And Southern defense of states' rights perversely fed the arguments of antislavery spokesmen, who used them to reject any extension of federal power protecting slave interests. Caught in this quandry, Virginia's Senator Mason asserted that the right to hold property in slaves was absolute and precedent to all other rights. Strange doctrine from the home state of Thomas Jefferson! Equally ironically, the doctrine of absolute right could be turned around by antislavery men who claimed that Christian teaching and moral law established a "higher law" which forbade their returning refugees from slavery. And if the higher law overshadowed constitutional obligation in the North, Southerners threatened to meet its challenge in ways equally unconstitutional. Once again it was Mason who warned that if a new fugitive law did not provide slaveowners adequate protection he would recommend that his fellow Southerners "provide by law for reprisals upon the property of the citizens of any offending State," concluding, "I know of no other mode of redress against those who acknowledge no obligation either of honor or of law"[19] (Document I-E-1). And at the extreme fringe of constitutional challenge R. Barnwell Rhett of South Carolina posed the ultimate solution of disunion. He urged Congress to repeal federal fugitive slave legislation and thus test the Northern states' will to meet their constitutional commitments. If they failed to act on their own, Rhett concluded, the disunion that would inevitably follow would be of their own making. Nothing would have pleased the most fanatic abolitionists more, for they too sought disunion and destruction of a constitution which protected slavery.

The New Fugitive Slave Law

Neither Southern nor Northern moderates, however, sought to strain the Constitution further but rather to preserve union. So in mid-September 1850, after eight months of almost continuous debate on all measures embodied in Clay's compromise, the Congress passed a fugitive slave bill which President Fillmore then signed. In substance it involved an extended roster of federal officials responsible for enforcing the return of fugitives, provided a simplified procedure for claimants, pressed private citizens—though not state officials—into its service, and in no way met Northern demands for judicial protection for alleged slaves. Specifically it empowered commissioners of federal circuit courts and persons specially appointed by the federal superior courts in the territories, as well as those courts themselves, to issue certificates entitling claimants of fugitive slaves to take their property back to the state or territory from which the slaves had fled, provided only that satisfactory proof was presented to such commissioner or other official that the prisoners were the fugitives as alleged and did owe service. The law charged federal marshals and their deputies to execute all warrants for the arrest of alleged fugitives issued by the commissioners and the courts and to be financially accountable should the fugitives escape. In pursuance of their duties, the marshals were authorized "to summon and call to their aid the bystanders, or *posse comitatus*."* But, should the claimant so prefer, he might seize a fugitive on his own responsibility without a warrant. Once the fugitive was seized, the law continued, an affidavit certified by any court in the state or territory from which the alleged slave had escaped was all that was required to establish the slave's identity and the fact that he owed service from which he had fled. If the fugitive met the affidavit's description, the commissioner or court was required to issue a certificate for his rendition. At

---

*A force of citizens conscripted by a sheriff or other legal officer to assist him in executing the law.

no time during this process was the alleged fugitive allowed to testify in his own behalf. And of course there was no provision for habeas corpus, jury trial, counsel, or the like.

The law also extended special aid against the dangers of illegal intervention to forestall the slave's return. Should the claimant or his attorneys file an affidavit after the certificate for return had been issued that a rescue attempt was anticipated, the marshal or other federal official holding the slave was "to remove him to the State whence he fled" at federal expense. Finally, those who obstructed the law were subject to a $1,000 fine and six months imprisonment and liable for an additional $1,000 damages should the owner bring civil suit. The federal government bore the expense of the usual fees for the marshal, deputies, and clerks unless the claimant failed to make good his claim. The commissioner was paid a $10 fee for his services if he found for the claimant, but only a $5 fee if he found against him.

By these terms slaveholders seemed to have gained strong new protection for their property. The financial arrangements, the terms of punishment, the nature of evidence required to establish legal grounds for the return of a fugitive, and the obligation imposed upon all citizens to assist in the capture and rendition of fugitives added force which the 1793 law had lacked. But even so, was it enforceable? Its very passage had been achieved only by the planned absenteeism of a large group of free state senators whose compromise consisted in not voting against the measure. North and South alike admitted that the law offended the mores and morals of many Northern communities. And even if the law could be enforced, would it curtail the property loss which border states experienced? Where slavery was least profitable as a labor system and least viable as an economic institution, would most owners undertake the expense of tracking down their runaways and employing agents and counsel to reclaim balky and unreliable servants?

Still and all, the Fugitive Slave Law of 1850 was of major importance to the South in its symbolic guarantees of property in slaves backed by the weight of the federal government. Its enactment alone confirmed the South's interpretation of the Constitution and the lasting nature of its sectional compromises. But if this symbol was to retain its meaning, then on those occasions when it was applied, it must be applied successfully. The federal government must demonstrate its resolution and firmness, and the North must comply if Henry Clay's compromise was to last. The line was drawn; the test was yet to come.

Notes

1. William Henry Seward, "Annual Message to the Legislature," January 7, 1840, in George Ellis Baker, ed., *Works of William H. Seward* (New York: Redfield, 1853-54), 2:221.

2. *16 Peters, Justice Story's Opinion*, 608, quoted in Marion Gleason McDougall, *Fugitive Slaves* (1891; New York: Bergman Publishers, 1967), 109.

3. George L. Clarke to Frederick Douglass, February 18, 1848, in *North Star*, March 3, 1948.

4. U.S., Congress, Senate, *Congressional Globe*, 31st Cong., 1st sess., January 16, 1850, 171.

5. *Ibid.*, 31st Cong., 1st sess., January 24, 1850, Appendix, 79.

6. *Ibid.*, 31st Cong., 1st sess., January 28, 1850, 233.

7. *Ibid.*, 31st Cong., 1st sess., August 19, 1850, Appendix, 1583.

8. *Ibid.*, 31st Cong., 1st sess., August 15, 1850, 1588.

9. Hudson Strode, *Jefferson Davis: American Patriot, 1808-1861* (New York: Harcourt, Brace and Co., 1955), 222.

10. William Henry Seward, *Speech on the Admission of California. Delivered in the Senate of the United States, March 11, 1850* (Washington: Buell and Blanchard, 1850), 17-18.

11. U.S., Congress, Senate, *Congressional Globe,* 31st Cong., 1st sess., August 19, 1850, Appendix, 1584.

12. *Ibid.*, 31st Cong., 1st sess., August 19, 1850, Appendix, 1585.

13. *Ibid.*, 31st Cong., 1st sess., August 20, 1850, Appendix, 1597.

14. Seward, *Admission of California,* 42.

15. U.S., Congress, Senate, *Congressional Globe,* 31st Cong., 1st sess., August 22, 1850, Appendix, 1614.

16. *Ibid.*, 31st Cong., 2nd sess., February 22, 1851, Appendix, 305.

17. Joshua R. Giddings, "Speech on the Annual Message of the President, of December, 1850. Delivered in Committee of whole House on the State of the Union, December 9, 1850," in *Speeches in Congress* (Boston: John P. Jewett and Company, 1853), 428-29.

18. William H. Seward to John A. Andrew, April 5, 1851, in *Liberator,* May 16, 1851.

19. U.S., Congress, Senate, *Congressional Globe,* 31st Cong., 1st sess., January 28, 1850, 236.

2

Administering the Law

Most Americans, both North and South, weary of the long debates on the Compromise of 1850 and hopeful of sectional peace, accepted the new fugitive slave law at face value. Observers generally sensed a new will to enforce the law and thus to end the dispute over slavery and save the Union. Political and civic leaders built support for it. "Let us then resolve," urged Pennsylvania Democrat James Buchanan, "to put down agitation at the North on the slave question, by the force of enlightened public opinion, and faithfully execute the provisions of the Fugitive Slave Law."[1] New York businessman John T. Brady admonished a public meeting called to support the new law that the Constitution and Union were a "mockery" unless all citizens upheld the law by an "efficient and thorough execution,"[2] and his auditors thereupon formed a Union Safety Committee for its support.

In such ways did public figures throughout the North respond to the South's early warnings that *the continued existence of the United States as one nation, depends upon the full and faithful execution of the Fugitive Slave Bill.*"[3] Various Southern state conventions in late 1850 and early 1851 repeated the sentiment. As Senator John Berrien of Georgia, in whose state union sentiment ran strong, told his fellow senators, should the North fail to enforce the law or should the federal government fail to press it, the nation faced grave danger.

Yet the enthusiasm of those who placed public order and law enforcement first faced opposition from the start. No sooner had the bill become law than petitions reached Congress seeking its repeal (Document I-B-2). They echoed familiar themes, that the law itself was both unfair and immoral, and roused Southern fears that a petition campaign similar to that of 1836 designed to rally Northern opposition to slavery was under way. Joshua Giddings, who had joined John Quincy Adams in his earlier campaign to receive all petitions respectfully, persistently introduced petitions from his Ohio constituents to the House of Representatives. Similarly, in the Senate William Seward was one of those who welcomed the opportunity to present repeal petitions.

But times had changed and the petition issue quickly fell behind antislavery events. The language of abolitionist attacks on the new law was no longer supplicatory but bristlingly defiant. Even before congressional debate on the bill had ended, groups in Massachusetts and New York had publicly urged disobedience and advised fugitives to arm themselves for self-defense. When the bill became law anguished abolitionists became still more militant (Document III-A-3). Indicative was the language of Syracuse Unitarian minister Samuel Joseph May, a thoroughgoing pacifist. "We must," wrote this gentle reformer, in a letter to Frederick Douglass's *North Star,* "trample this infamous law under foot, be the consequences what they may. Fines, imprisonment shall not deter me from doing what I can for the fugitive, and the sooner and the oftener we have trials of this law, the better."[4] In Boston, May's fellow Unitarian cleric, Theodore Parker, kept a loaded pistol in his desk, not because he sought violence, but because he was ready to do "all in my power to rescue any fugitive slave from the hands of any officer who attempts to return him to bondage."[5] Equally resolute, Massachusetts politician Charles Sumner implied a similar course at a Free Soil convention. "Individuals among us, as elsewhere," he concluded, "may forget humanity in a fancied loyalty to law; but the public conscience will not allow a man, who has trodden our streets as a freeman, to be dragged away as a slave."[6]

Blacks as well as whites openly challenged the new law (Document III-A-1 and 2). In mass meetings throughout the North they closed ranks, emphasizing less the abstract morality of a higher law than the imperatives of simple survival. "Shall we resist Oppression? Shall we defend our Liberties? Shall we be FREEMEN or SLAVES?" New York City Negroes asked, vowing "Should any one attempt to execute its provisions on any one of us, either by invading our home or arresting us in the street, we will treat such an one as assaulting our persons with intent to kill, and, God being our helper, will use such means as will repel the aggressor and defend our lives and liberty."[7] Buffalo blacks determined to fight, as far as they could, "every attempt to enforce any act by which an American citizen is liable to be deprived of life or liberty without due process of law, without a trial by a jury of his peers, or without the privilege of the writ of habeas corpus."[8] In Boston, Negroes rejected the alternative of fleeing to Canada and urged their brethren to stay in the United States amid "tears, toils, and perils" and struggle to make America "truly 'the land of the free and the home of the brave.' "[9] To give force to their resolve, blacks from Maine to Illinois formed new vigilance committees and revitalized old ones to "give direction," as the Portland, Maine, group said, "to whatever measures may be necessary for our protection."[10]

Testing the Law

While these protests were broached, the South, the beneficiary of the new law, stood willing, for a time, to let the matter rest. "Most men [in the South] were weary of strife," historian Avery Craven has written. "They wanted things to work out well, and the wishful thinking was enough to go on for the present."[11] Yet only to a point. They tolerated Northern defiance so long as it remained verbal. But when professions of higher law and moral obligation were converted into overt acts to evade the law, tolerance quickly diminished.

Boston, in the Southern mind the focus of antislavery activity, gave the law its first major test. Even before February 15, 1851, when the Shadrach case broke, the city had seen the law thwarted. William and Ellen Craft, whose escape from Georgia with Ellen impersonating William's white master had been widely publicized, were in town when the fugitive bill became law. With their arrest under it already in preparation, abolitionists hastily sent them off to England. Thus it seemed imperative to federal officials that the first full-fledged application of the law in Boston be successful.

In mid-February, then, John Caphart of Norfolk, Virginia, obtained from Commissioner George T. Curtis an arrest warrant for Frederick Wilkins, popularly known as Shadrach. Still smarting from the Craft affair, deputy federal marshal Patrick Riley carefully staked out the Cornhill Coffee House where Wilkins was a waiter. Then on Saturday morning, February 15, he and his men arrested the black man. Word of the arrest spread quickly, and within hours five well-known Boston lawyers volunteered as counsel for the defendant. To give them time to develop their case, Curtis granted a delay in the hearings until the following Tuesday.

Up to that point all had gone according to script, despite the fact that Marshal Riley had no place to keep his prisoner other than the courthouse, where the federal government rented courtroom space. Denied by Massachusetts law the use of any state jails for holding a fugitive slave, Riley was made doubly insecure by the mayor's refusal of special police protection at the courthouse and the commander of the Boston naval yard's refusal to use his facilities for Shadrach's safekeeping. His legitimate fears for his prisoner's incarceration were, however, short-circuited in a most unexpected manner. After Curtis had granted the delay, the courtroom gradually emptied. The lawyers and commissioner had already left when suddenly a door burst open and a crowd of blacks, pushing Riley and his men aside, swarmed into the room, encompassed Wilkins, and swept him out the opposite door. When next heard from, Wilkins was safe in Montreal.

Marshal Riley's careful preparations and official Washington's sharp response to Wilkins's escape strongly suggest that his arrest was intended to demonstrate a firm federal intention to enforce the law regardless of Northern opposition. The executive branch had made its concern clear. Only a month after he signed the bill into law, President Fillmore had pledged himself to enforce it faithfully as part of his constitutional duty. Two months later, in his first annual message, he called on all Americans to obey the law as the only way to insure that American government remained one of laws, not of men. If the law offended, it must be repealed legally, not defied (Document II-A-1).

The rescue, however, cast doubt on this resolution. Within three days Congress had considered the matter and called for the relevant executive documents. The president, in turn, used this opportunity to elaborate his views. By February 18, he had already ordered all federal civil and military officers to aid in Wilkins's recapture and simultaneously had directed the government to prosecute those who had aided and abetted the escape. Then, in his message to Congress which accompanied these documents, Fillmore went on to condemn Massachusetts's personal liberty laws and especially its denial of state jail facilities in fugitive cases. Because of that state's uncooperativeness, he sought congressional action to empower him to call the state militia into federal service without the time-consuming proclamation process which existing law required (Document II-B-1).

Congressional assessment of the Shadrach case varied. Kentucky Whig Henry Clay saw in it an invitation to a strong law-and-order stand. Though he also noted that it involved a black threat to white dominance, the thrust of his argument lay elsewhere. "If to-day the law upon the subject of fugitive slaves is obstructed by violence and force, and its execution prevented, what other law on our statute-book may not to-morrow be obstructed by equal violence and its execution prevented? What department of the Government," Clay continued fervently, "what Government itself, will not be opposed by violence and by force, and thus its very existence be threatened?"[12] Across the aisle, Iowa Senator Augustus Caesar Dodge had already seconded his more famous colleague's sentiments. "I am . . . in favor of steps being taken such as will at the threshold stop all resistance to the law."[13]

Antislavery senator John Hale of New Hampshire, on the other hand, thought the president had blown the Shadrach affair out of all proportion. It was, he said, nothing more than a "momentary impulse to successful resistance to law," common to all civilizations at all times. The reaction of the government, he warned, was excessive. "If upon every such occasion such a parade as this is made, it will bring the Government into contempt. . . . Instead of strengthening, you weaken; instead of giving respect, you take it away"[14] (Document II-C-2).

Southern senators denied Hale's analysis. Many saw in the rescue evidence of a larger conspiracy, "the acting out of a great and widely-spread scheme throughout no small portion of New England,"[15] as North Carolina Senator George Badger said. Senator Hopkins Turney of Tennessee claimed that closely knit groups or "clubs" of antislavery Northerners stayed constantly on the alert to frustrate the law. And Stephen Douglas of Illinois, prime promoter of the 1850 compromise, agreed with these conclusions. For others the rescue bespoke less a conspiracy against the law than its basic inutility. Senator Butler, a strong supporter of the Mason bill, now agreed with Jefferson Davis that the law was futile (Document I-C-2). Only military force, Butler thought, could enforce it. The crux was, as Davis had said, that "there was not a sentiment in the northern States to enforce the law, and without that public sentiment, without that consent . . . the law was useless"[16] (Document II-C-1).

These critiques did not, however, shake Fillmore's determination to enforce the law and vindicate the 1850 compromise. He assigned Daniel Webster, the strongest member of his cabinet, to coordinate the prosecution of the Shadrach case. Richard Henry Dana, counsel for several of the defendants, learned from the federal district attorney that it was Webster who called the moves in the various trials and who would not drop the matter even after the jury refused to convict in several cases.

Webster's course could have been predicted from his public statements. In May 1851, for instance, he told an Albany, New York, audience that the fugitive slave law was "fair, reasonable, equitable, and just" and gave "the

Southern States what they were entitled to, and what it was intended originally they should receive."[17] But he also went beyond support for the 1850 compromise to excoriate those who had already chosen to set the law at naught. Verbal opposition fell within the boundaries of free speech, but action on such opposition was, he asserted, nothing short of treason. Thus Webster's and Fillmore's determination to punish the Shadrach rescuers was not only a question of enforcing one unpopular law but of punishing traitors who threatened the national existence.

A month before Webster's Albany address, Boston had presented the Fillmore administration another opportunity to show that it could enforce the fugitive law. On the night of April 3, young Thomas Sims, recently arrived from Savannah, Georgia, was arrested in the city. This time federal officials secured the full cooperation of the municipal government, in a distinct change from the Wilkins episode. City policemen, hastily sworn in as deputy federal marshals, made the arrest. Whig mayor, John P. Bigelow, and city police chief, Francis Tukey, largely ignored state law in their efforts to assist federal authorities. Once Sims was in custody, the police strung chains waist-high about the courthouse to hold back the crowds and forestall rescue attempts. For the nine days that Sims remained there, the courthouse was a jail, constantly patrolled by city police. That this violated the letter and spirit of Massachusetts's personal liberty law was of no apparent significance. Thomas Higginson, a young abolitionist and no impartial observer, reported that Chief Tukey had even admitted to "violating the state law"; but, Tukey contended, "I am acting under orders, and it is the major and the aldermen who are responsible."[18] Moreover, in April 1851, city officials had widespread citizen support for their actions.

Thus nearly everything conspired against Sims. As was true in the Wilkins case, the fugitive did have distinguished counsel, including Democratic Congressman Robert Rantoul, Jr., who, basing his moves on his interpretation of states' rights in slavery matters, sought state aid in protecting Sims. But despite the state's well-known antislavery sympathies, Massachusetts officials denied Rantoul's requests. State Chief Justice Lemuel Shaw refused to issue a writ of habeas corpus precisely because he wished to avoid a showdown between state and federal power. Then, when a lower state court sought to have Sims remanded to its custody on criminal charges arising from the assault Sims had committed in resisting arrest, the federal marshal refused to surrender him even though criminal charges customarily took precedence over civil procedures. And even had the matter been pressed, it would probably have stumbled on federal district attorney Benjamin Hallett's determination to retain custody of Sims by pressing federal criminal charges, which took precedence over the state charges. Foiled in their efforts to achieve state action, Sims's attorneys subsequently sought a writ of habeas corpus from federal judges on the grounds that Sims had then been held beyond the legal time limit set for examining a prisoner and that the warrant for his arrest was technically defective. These moves too were denied first by Judge Peleg Sprague and, on appeal, by Judge Levi Woodbury.

As legal recourse failed, so too did illegal rescue. Those blacks who had saved Wilkins two months earlier had largely fled the city to avoid prosecution, leaving too few to undertake a similar attempt for Sims. And white abolitionists, though they concocted several plans, failed to devise a workable one. So Thomas Sims was returned South, with little local disturbance and much support.

President Fillmore was delighted. "I congratulate you and the country," he wrote to Webster, "upon a triumph of law in Boston. She has done nobly. She has wiped out the stain of the former rescue [of Wilkins] and freed herself from the reproach of nullification."[19]

Forcible Resistance

In some other fugitive cases, however, the administration was less successful. Early in September 1851, Maryland slaveholder Edward Gorsuch, accompanied by a federal marshal, arrived in the southeastern Pennsylvania village of Christiana to reclaim four escaped slaves. Warned in advance of his approach, the fugitives hid in the house of William Parker, where other local blacks rallied to their protection. Not to be deterred, Gorsuch and his associates persisted until a gun battle occurred in which Gorsuch was killed and his son gravely wounded. When it was all over the four fugitives had disappeared, and Parker fled to Canada.

Once again the federal government acted to punish where it had not prevented. Some fifty marines were dispatched to Christiana where they turned the local hotel into a jail and courthouse from which the affair was investigated. Several weeks later, acting on Webster's conception of the offence, the government obtained indictments against some forty participants, not for violation of the Fugitive Slave Law but on charges of treason. Only one of them, Castner Hanway, a local white Quaker, was tried, and he was acquitted. Failing to win the first case, the federal district attorney George W. Ashmead dropped the treason charges against the others and sought no further indictments on lesser grounds. Thus once again the Fugitive Slave Law had been successfully challenged.

After the Christiana affair but before the trials, yet another successful defiance of the law occurred at Syracuse in upstate New York. There on October 1 Jerry McHenry was arrested as a fugitive. Both the timing and the locale suggested to many that Webster was seeking another dramatic demonstration that the government could and would enforce the law. Syracuse lay not only in the heart of politically oriented antislavery country but was also a major transfer point on the Underground Rail Road, efficiently overseen by two clergymen, white Samuel J. May and black Jarmain Loguen. Taking a fugitive there would strike at a major flight route to Canada. But McHenry had been in Syracuse for some time and was well known to its inhabitants. Why then did federal officials select him and choose October 1 for the arrest, just when the local agricultural fair and a Liberty party regional convention brought mobs of people to town, many of them abolitionists?

The evidence suggests either careless ineptitude or a careful choice to draw attention to the case.

Immediately after McHenry's arrest, a battery of lawyers offered counsel and were present at the preliminary hearing which began that same afternoon. When the proceedings recessed at about two-thirty, a group of blacks made their way into the court room, snatched up McHenry, and rushed him out, much as Boston blacks had done in the Shadrach rescue. They failed, however, to meld into the crowds, and police pursued them down the streets, around corners, and over a bridge. Finally the chase ended with the fugitive again in the hands of the police, who returned him to the Justice House. There he was placed under close guard. At five o'clock the hearings resumed, and at seven o'clock recessed until the following morning. Meanwhile, however, Unitarian minister May and Liberty party leader Gerrit Smith had planned a second rescue. At nine o'clock that evening the milling crowd, which had been throwing stones at the Justice House, invaded it, drove back the guards, freed McHenry and carried him victoriously on their shoulders to Bratnell's Hotel. There he was hurried away in a carriage, hidden for several days, and finally delivered across the lake to Canada.

In hindsight sober citizens speculated on the melodrama of McHenry's arrest and escape. The Syracuse *Journal* was sure that with care and efficiency the unpopular Fugitive Slave Law could be enforced in the city. Positing that "there would have been no disturbance, and [that] any attempt at a rescue would have been frustrated" had the government been able to "inspire the public with respect" or "been capable of managing a matter of this importance with judgment and wisdom,"[20] the newspaper blamed federal authorities for botching the whole affair. Testimony to their failure was the sole injury of the day, the broken arm of a marshal who, in fleeing the mob, had jumped from a window.

Once again federal resolution stiffened after the event—this time in a series of trials which lasted for nearly two years. Once again the district attorney laid treason charges against the leaders, including May and Smith, who were arraigned in nearby Auburn, home town of William Seward. There the senator went bond for their bail, entertained them, and agreed to act as defense counsel should his services be necessary. But in mid-November, when the government sought indictments from a grand jury on the treason charges, it was rebuffed. Not won over by the logic of Webster's treason theory, the grand jurors returned indictments merely for participating in riot and obstructing the return of a fugitive.

No previous fugitive slave case had been so clearly politicized, and Seward's willingness to enter the case said as much. Presumably the government's reluctance to try the two self-confessed rescuers reflected its fear that Seward would follow through. May, who had concluded to use his trial as a platform from which to challenge the law's unconstitutionality and "egregious wickedness," was bitterly disappointed when neither his nor Smith's indictment was pressed.[21] But charges of political motives went still further. John Thomas, editor of a Liberty party paper, claimed that Webster himself had drawn the original indictments and insisted that the success of the prosecution would determine whether President Fillmore would seek a second term. Whether Thomas's charges were true or not, the president was troubled politically by the effects of the Jerry, Gorsuch, and Shadrach cases. In his annual message of December 1851 he emphasized again a determination to enforce the law. Like Webster he saw in opposition to it more than simple lawbreaking. Those who disobeyed it attacked the Constitution and thereby betrayed "their wish to see that Constitution overturned." If his administration was to prevent potential traitors from "rend[ing] asunder this Union,"[22] it had to take action. Yet what could it do? Not only had it failed to prevent three spectacular rescues; it had had little success in punishing the transgressors. In both the Shadrach and Christiana cases no one was found guilty on federal charges; and in the Jerry prosecutions only one defendant, Enoch Reed, a black man, was convicted, and that not under the controversial 1850 law but under the old 1793 statute. Of the other Jerry defendants who reached trial, two were set free by hung juries and one was acquitted; the cases against all the rest were finally abandoned.

While the government pressed its enforcement program with minimal success, abolitionists continued to attack the new law. Abby Kelley Foster, a most ardent agitator, concluded shortly after the Shadrach rescue that "the U. States Government . . . must be wholly abolished or entirely modified" if slavery was to be ended (Document III-B-1). The 1850 law was, she thought, "the last ounce of aggression" the American people would tolerate.[23] For Thomas Wentworth Higginson, the government's excessive measures in guarding the courthouse during the Sims case helped the cause, for such blatant use of force made "abolitionists very fast."[24] And Samuel J. May took satisfaction not only in freeing Jerry McHenry but in bringing "the people into direct conflict with the Government" and thus opposing its "grossest abuses" of power.[25]

Compelled for years to fight slavery indirectly and at a distance, abolitionists now had an immediate object for head-on attack. Following Sims's rendition, Garrison, formerly an absolute nonresistant, backed armed opposition to law. "If 'resistance to tyrants,' by bloody weapons, 'is obedience to God . . . ,'"he challenged a meeting commemorating Sims's return, "then every fugitive slave is justified in arming himself for protection and defence,—in taking the life of every marshal, commissioner, or other person who attempts to reduce him to bondage."[26] In Syracuse "Jerry rescue" commemorations became annual events. At the first anniversary, a throng of 5,000 or more people, denied the use of city hall, assembled in the new engine house of the Syracuse and Utica Rail Road to celebrate successful defiance of law. The new mood was nowhere better defined, however, than in an 1851 resolution of the American Anti-Slavery Society. "As for the Fugitive Slave Law, we execrate it, we spit upon it, we trample it under our feet."[27]

The Politics of Repeal

The conflict over early attempts to enforce the Fugitive Slave Law also marked election-year politics in 1852. In the Congress, while they recognized its practical futility, antislavery legislators repeatedly raised the question of repeal, though they frequently had to stretch a point to relate their remarks to the topic directly under debate. The only major speech for repeal, however, came from Massachusetts's new senator, Charles Sumner.

On July 27, 1852, Sumner had tried to treat the matter directly by offering a resolution for repeal. Immediately Senator James Shields of Illinois denounced the proposal as "treasonable"[28] ; and Walter Brooke of Mississippi solemnly warned that any motion for repeal would be construed by both his state and Georgia as a "sufficient cause for the dissolution of this Union."[29] Denied the privilege of making his proposal by a three-to-one vote, Sumner bided his time. On August 26 he saw his chance. Robert M.T. Hunter of Virginia had just proposed to amend a general appropriations bill so as to authorize paying the "extraordinary expenses" incurred in the process of enforcing any federal law. The amendment's purpose, though not so stated, was to cover expenses incurred under the Fugitive Slave Law. At once Sumner offered an amendment to Hunter's denying its application to that law; and, burying it in a subordinate clause, Sumner included the provision that the much hated law was "hereby repealed."[30]

Thus had Sumner created an opening for his attack on the fugitive law. No one could limit his speaking directly to the business of the Senate; so he launched a three-and-three-quarter-hour carefully structured and well-memorized oration. Slavery, he argued, was exclusively a matter for state responsibility. The return of fugitives, therefore, could not constitutionally be undertaken by the federal government. To the contrary, each state must decide how to meet its obligation and could approach the problem from the assumptions of a free rather than a slave state. The only clear-cut restraint on state action was the constitutional requirement that it not legislate freedom for fugitives bound to service in other states (Document I-E-2). The debate which followed showed clearly that Sumner's intent was less letting each state take responsibility for returning fugitives than rendering the constitutional provision for such return inoperative.

Although Sumner's amendment won only four votes, its overwhelming defeat reflected less the convictions of Northern senators than the imperatives of election-year politics. With few exceptions, senators could not appear loyal to their party's platform and also support the Massachusetts senator. On the other hand, for Free Soilers like John P. Hale, the party's presidential candidate, it was easy because his party's platform read "that the Fugitive Slave Act of 1850 is repugnant to the Constitution, to the principles of the common law, to the spirit of Christianity, and to the sentiments of the civilized world."[31] Sumner was only proposing to realize their common party's goal.

But for antislavery Whigs the choice was not so easy. Members of a national party, they were caught in the constraints of practical politics. Though they were not enchanted by the Whig presidential candidate, Winfield Scott, they hoped he could be elected and that as president, they could control him. Their party's platform, however, reflected Fillmore's loyalty to the 1850 Compromise and his determination to enforce the Fugitive Slave

Law. Explicitly rejecting repeal, its only sop to the law's opponents was an oblique reference to alteration at some indeterminate future date.

For Democrats there was even less latitude. Their platform fully supported the fugitive law as a permanent and constitutionally binding obligation. Although their presidential candidate, New Hampshire's Franklin Pierce, had once indiscretely confessed his dislike for the law, his public record belied the slightest antislavery tinge. From 1836, when as a young congressman he had supported the Gag resolution against receiving antislavery petitions, he set the course he thereafter followed, supporting the Southern wing of his party. In 1850 he had forced the Democratic gubernatorial candidate in New Hampshire to resign after the latter had repudiated the Fugitive Slave Law. Later Pierce persuaded both his state party convention and a state constitutional convention to endorse the 1850 Compromise and particularly the fugitive law (Document II-A-2).

Despite lingering doubts among some Southerners that he might not be wholly sound on the fugitive slave question—and his preelection correspondence indicates that that was one of three major issues raised against him during the campaign—his past record met the challenge. When the votes were counted Pierce had a 200,000 majority over Scott, while the total Free Soil vote amounted to less than 157,000. Pierce saw in the election tally a talisman of sectional harmony and a mandate for vigorous enforcement of the fugitive law. To Horace Greeley, antislavery editor of the New York *Tribune*, the election meant roughly the same thing. "There is no probability," he wrote, "that . . . the Fugitive Slave Law . . . will be altered by Congress during the present generation."[32] The desire for harmony seemed to have triumphed over the higher law.

Notes

1. From a speech of November 19, 1850, quoted in Stanley W. Campbell, *The Slave Catchers: Enforcement of the Fugitive Slave Law, 1850-1860* (Chapel Hill: University of North Carolina Press, 1970), 107.

2. Quoted in *ibid.*, 74.

3. John R. Thompson, writing in the *Southern Literary Messenger* (1850), quoted in Avery O. Craven, *The Growth of Southern Nationalism, 1848-1861* (Baton Rouge: Louisiana State University Press, 1953), 104.

4. Reprinted in *Liberator*, October 25, 1850.

5. Theodore Parker, "The Function of Conscience," in *The Slave Power*, vol. XI of James K. Hosmer, ed., *The Centenary Edition [of the Works of Theodore Parker]* (Boston: American Unitarian Association, n.d.), 304.

6. U.S., Congress, Senate, *Congressional Globe*, 32nd Cong., 1st sess., October 3, 1850, Appendix, 1116.

7. *National Anti-Slavery Standard*, October 10, 1850.

8. *Impartial Citizen*, October 12, 1850.

9. *Ibid.*, October 12, 1850.

10. *Liberator*, November 1, 1850.

11. Craven, *Growth of Southern Nationalism*, 122.

12. U.S., Congress, Senate, *Congressional Globe*, 31st Cong., 2nd sess., February 24, 1851, Appendix, 321.

13. *Ibid.*, 31st Cong., 2nd sess., February 22, 1851, Appendix, 310.

14. *Ibid.*, 31st Cong., 2nd sess., February 21, 1851, Appendix, 296.

15. *Ibid.*, 31st Cong., 2nd sess., February 21, 1851, Appendix, 301.

16. *Ibid.*, 31st Cong., 2nd sess., February 18, 1851, 598.

17. Daniel Webster, *Works* (7th edition. Boston: Little, Brown and Co., 1853), 2:575.

18. Quoted in Roger Lane, *Policing the City, Boston 1822-1885* (Cambridge: Harvard University Press, 1967), 74.

19. Millard Fillmore to Daniel Webster, April 16, 1851, quoted in Campbell, *Slave Catchers,* 99-100.

20. Syracuse *Journal,* n.d., reprinted in *Frederick Douglass' Paper,* October 9, 1851.

21. Samuel J. May to William Lloyd Garrison, November 23, 1851, in Wendell Phillips Garrison and Francis Jackson Garrison, *William Lloyd Garrison, 1805-1879. The Story of His Life Told by His Children* (Boston: Houghton Mifflin, 1885-89), 3:336.

22. James D. Richardson, comp., *A Compilation of the Messages and Papers of the Presidents. . .* (New York: Bureau of National Literature, 1897-1917), 6:2674.

23. *National Anti-Slavery Standard,* April 3, 1851.

24. Thomas W. Higginson to [Newburyport *Union*], Fast Day, [1851], in Thomas W. Higginson, comp., Ms Correspondence, etc., Relating to the Anthony Burns Episode, etc., 1851-1900. Antislavery Collection, Boston Public Library.

25. Samuel J. May to William Lloyd Garrison, November 23, 1851; Antislavery Collection, Boston Public Library.

26. Wendell Phillips, *Speeches, Lectures, and Letters* (Boston: J. Redpath, 1863), 71.

27. *National Anti-Slavery Standard,* May 15, 1851.

28. U.S. Congress, Senate, *Congressional Globe,* 32nd Cong., 1st sess., July 28, 1852, 1952.

29. *Ibid.*, 32nd Cong., 1st sess., July 28, 1852, 1950.

30. *Ibid.*, 32nd Cong., 1st sess., August 26, 1852, Appendix, 1102.

31. Kirk H. Porter and Donald Bruce Johnson, *National Party Platforms, 1840-1956* (Urbana: University of Illinois Press, 1956), 18.

32. Quoted in Campbell, *Slave Catchers,* 79.

3

The Burns Crisis

At his inaugural in March 1852, the new president, Franklin Pierce, expressed his hope for a lasting Union and urged an end to agitation of the slavery issue. He pledged himself to uphold the Compromise of 1850 with its guarantees of Southern slavery which all Americans were bound to respect. Especially did he admonish his fellow Northerners to obey these laws "not with a reluctance encouraged by abstract opinions as to their propriety in a different state of society, but cheerfully and according to the decisions of the tribunal to which their exposition belongs."[1] In this spirit the Pierce administration vowed to act.

From the outset, however, Pierce disregarded elementary political tactics needed to achieve his goals. Committed to uphold the compromise firmly, he needed the advice and support of prominent Unionists, both Northern and Southern. Yet instead of appointing such men to major posts, Pierce chose, in the words of historian Allen Nevins, "to be bland, conciliatory, and yielding";[2] trying to satisfy all factions and thereby to achieve the stasis and tranquility he sought. Still worse, his cabinet not only contained no strong Southern unionist but also lacked any Northern antislavery balance for its nascent secessionists.

Indeed the cabinet was a strange amalgam. Secretary of War, Jefferson Davis of Mississippi, was the only Southern member of major stature. Self-appointed heir of John C. Calhoun, Davis had opposed the Compromise of 1850 and thought the Fugitive Slave Law a delusive substitute for Southern equality in the territories. His potential counterweight was William L. Marcy, an aging New Yorker who, though not a Barnburner, had some support from his state's free soil Democrats. However, although he backed the 1850 Compromise and was personally unsympathetic to slavery, as Secretary of State, Marcy confined his interests mostly to foreign affairs. The only other notable in the cabinet was Caleb Cushing, the Attorney General, trusted by no one. A Massachusetts Whig turned Democrat, he had as a young congressman in the 1830s supported John Quincy Adams's efforts to receive antislavery petitions. Never an abolitionist, however, he moved into the Democratic party during the 1840s and by 1850 identified himself with its Southern wing. Thus of Pierce's three principal cabinet advisors, Marcy, the most experienced politician, lacked the stamina to be involved in domestic issues; Davis was a relative newcomer with little exposure on the national scene; and Cushing lacked a political following even in his own state.

With these three men at its center, the cabinet offered little strength to a dark horse and undistinguished president. Nor was Pierce any better off in his relations with Congress. Starting with no close and influential contacts in either house, he frittered his small influence away with a patronage policy which satisfied no faction by trying to pacify all. Moreover, Pierce made no attempt to set a legislative course for Congress. His first annual message was best characterized by his biographer, Roy Nichols, as indecisive, presenting Congress not with an administrative program but with "an orthodox Democratic President's creed, which they might find useful as a standard of party and Congressional action."[3] Within the month, Congress had already begun to destroy the goal which Pierce had set for his presidency—national harmony based on no further agitation of the slavery issue.

In January 1854 Democratic Senator Stephen Douglas of Illinois introduced the bill that eventually became the Kansas-Nebraska Act. In his proposal to organize this part of the Louisiana purchase into two territories, Douglas left the question of slavery's status in the projected states to the decision of their resident voters. By resorting thus to popular sovereignty, Douglas closely followed the pattern of the 1850 Compromise for Utah and New Mexico. But in so doing, he seemed to cast the 1820 Compromise, governing slavery in the Louisiana purchase, into limbo. Before long Whig Senator Archibald Dixon of Kentucky made this implication explicit by offering an amendment specifically repealing that part of the Missouri Compromise which had barred slavery north of 36° 30'. Unwilling to give the opposition party credit for extending the area open to slavery, Southern Democrats at once made Dixon's amendment their own and demanded Douglas's support for it if he was to have their support for the rest of the bill.

Caught in the political manoeuvres of his own party, Pierce lacked the strength and imagination to hold it to its commitment to avoid reopening the slavery question. Pressured by Senate Democratic leaders, Pierce gave in to their demands and made the Nebraska bill, with its amendment, an administration measure. Indeed he even drafted the final version of the amendment, which stated that the Compromise of 1850 had superceded the Missouri Compromise and left it "inoperative and void," so that slavery in all the territories was subject to popular sovereignty.

Northerners immediately branded Pierce a traitor to the principles of compromise he had earlier espoused, and he made no attempt to mollify them. In fact, although the first of the Jerry rescue trials had ended with only a single conviction nearly a month before he took office, the new president would not let the matter drop, and six months later the administration reopened the Jerry case. At first antislavery rumor claimed that Attorney General Cushing himself would lead the prosecution with new charges of conspiracy directed principally against Samuel J. May and Gerrit Smith, admitted plotters of the successful rescue. Apparently, however, the government had second thoughts and quickly backed off. The observations of the Albany *Evening Journal* after the first Jerry trials suggest at least one good reason for the decision. "The Government has begun to discover," it had commented in February, "that its trials of the 'Rescuers' has done more to impair the efficiency of the Fugitive Slave Law, than would have been done, if a gang of fifty 'Jerries' had marched up State Street, in broad daylight, on their unmolested road to Canada."[4]

That the decision marked no compromise with abolitionist sentiment, the attorney general's subsequent course demonstrated. In September 1853, for example, Cushing conveyed to Massachusetts Democrats the president's disapproval of their contemplated coalition with Free Soilers in the forthcoming state elections. "If there be any purpose more fixed than another in the mind of the President and those with whom he is accustomed to consult," he wrote to the Boston *Post*, "it is that the dangerous element of Abolitionism, under whatever guise or form it may present itself, shall be crushed out, so far as his administration is concerned."[5] Shortly thereafter, the attorney general advised the president that the government could and should pay the legal expenses of a federal marshal sued in an Indiana court for falsely arresting an alleged fugitive. In so doing he stressed the chief executive's duty to execute "the acts of Congress for the inter-state extradition of fugitives from service, in the face of organized combinations to defeat or resist that execution, and to harass those engaged in it, by vexatious suits or other unlawful or unjust contrivances."[6] And in March 1854, the president ordered the attorney general to impress on Marshal Watson Freeman in Massachusetts his duty to enforce the Fugitive Slave Law more efficiently.

Pierce, like Fillmore before him, sought vigorous implementation of the fugitive law, especially in Massachusetts. His reasons were clear. Boston was the home of Garrison's *Liberator* and the headquarters of the American Anti-Slavery Society. It was a hub of reform activity and the agitation which went with it. As Iowa's Senator Dodge put it after the Shadrach rescue, Boston was "the great abolition head-quarters—the theatre upon which agitators, whether natives or foreigners, carry on their operations against the domestic peace and quiet of the country."[7] That Cushing, like Webster, came from Massachusetts only increased the administration's determination to make its capital symbolic of the law's enforcement rather than of successful defiance.

Moreover, after 1851, the abrasive behavior of Senator Charles Sumner drew attention to the state as, with great learning and a vocabulary ranging from the scholarly to the scabrous, he unceasingly attacked the whole slave system. While a member of the Massachusetts General Court, Cushing had fought against Sumner's election to the Senate, and his opposition was amply vindicated by Sumner's course in Washington. In his August 1852 speech supporting the repeal of the Fugitive Slave Law, the new senator charged that only upheaval and turpitude resulted from enforcing the law. "Rage, tumult, commotion, mob, riot, violence, [and] death gush from its fatal overflowing fountains." Accusing those who applied this law of inhumanity, he asserted that "the spirit of the law passes into them, as the devils entered the swine. Upstart commissioners, the mere mushrooms of courts, vie and revie with each other. Now, by indecent speed, now by harshness of manner, now by a denial of evidence, now by crippling the defense, and now by open, glaring wrong, they make the odious act yet more odious."[8]

His language as well as its substance earned Sumner enemies other than Cushing. Dodge of Iowa charged him with seeking either bloody revolution, or still worse, racial equality; and John Weller of California agreed. George

Badger of North Carolina deplored Sumner's arrogance and abusiveness as much as his object. "I have sometimes heard speeches here," the North Carolinian told his colleagues, "which have, I confess, caused me deep regret; but this wholesale and revolting denunciation of a public law, and epithets applied to it, and to every person connected with the passing of it, is without example in our past history, and I trust in God it will never be followed in future."[9] Clearly the state which sent such a man to the Senate needed correction.

By the perversity of human events, brought about either by chance or intent, the determination to enforce the Fugitive Slave Law in Massachusetts and the revocation of the Missouri Compromise by the Kansas-Nebraska Act coincided almost exactly. By May 1854, abolitionists long critical of all compromises with slavery found themselves defending the 1820 Compromise. At the same time Cotton Whigs who had staked economic interest, personal and political careers, and sheer good faith on Unionist compromise reeled back at the betrayal of the Kansas-Nebraska Act. Two months before the bill became law, Unionist cotton textile magnate Amos A. Lawrence had warned Boston Congressman William Appleton that passage of the bill would "operate at once against the Southern interest viz the complete nullification of the Fugitive Slave Law. No slave," he predicted, "can be captured in a Northern state after this bill is passed."[10]

Nonetheless, when the bill cleared the House on May 24, Boston Democrats fired a 113 gun salute to celebrate the 113 Democratic and Whig votes which passed the act. That same evening at eight o'clock, three officers, deputized by U.S. Marshal Watson Freeman and carrying a warrant issued by Fugitive Slave Commissioner Edward G. Loring, seized Anthony Burns as he walked home from work.

The Abolitionist Response

Antislavery Boston responded at once. The Reverend Leonard Grimes, told of the arrest by Burns's employer, secondhand clothing dealer Coffin Pitts, quickly spread the word. Next morning the well-known black lawyer Robert Morris, Charles M. Ellis, a young antislavery attorney, and Richard Henry Dana, who had been one of Frederick Wilkins's counsel and had taken part in the legal efforts to free Thomas Sims, were on hand at the courthouse to defend Burns. But Burns, Dana reported, was unsure of accepting counsel. "Completely cowed and dispirited,"[11] the fugitive feared that fighting his arrest might result in harsh treatment were he returned to Virginia.

His fear was not unreasonable, for Anthony Burns had enjoyed singular advantages as a slave. Hired out from early childhood by his master, Charles Suttle, shopkeeper, small-time politician, and militia colonel of Alexandria, Burns had benefited from the relative freedom such an arrangement allowed. He had learned to read and write, had joined a church and become a preacher. His varied work experiences as personal servant, sawmill worker (in which trade he mangled his hand), and tavern servant increased his job options and relative independence. Eventually sent to Richmond, Burns not only hired his own time but supervised the hiring out of four other slaves belonging to Suttle. Though he still technically reported to Suttle's agent, William Brent, Burns's life in Richmond was essentially his own. He was hired to a druggist, but in slack time, took other jobs, merely paying his principal employer a stipulated fee for the privilege. Like many other slaves who lived and worked in urban areas, Burns enjoyed great freedom. Nonetheless he took the opportunity to escape aboard a northbound vessel when he had the chance.

Burns's special advantages, however, proved his undoing in Boston. Able to write, he corresponded with his brother, still a slave of Colonel Suttle, who intercepted the letter and immediately left for Boston to reclaim his slave. Shortly after his arrest Burns was confronted by his old master and Brent, who had accompanied him. Here he made his second mistake. Addressing Suttle by name, acknowledging his slave status, and making the excuse that he had come North inadvertently after having fallen asleep while working aboard a boat as a stevedore, Burns in fact admitted to his unauthorized journey to Boston.

In the circumstance, docile submission had a good deal to commend it; a decision to fight his master in court promised only disaster if Burns lost. Richard Dana appreciated the dilemma. When the hearing began he approached the bench and sought a delay on the ground that Burns needed time to decide whether he wished counsel. Commissioner Loring, no political hack but a distinguished lawyer, probate judge, and lecturer at Harvard Law School, granted the delay, and adjourned the proceedings until Saturday morning, May 27, two days hence.

By the following afternoon Burns had chosen to be represented by Dana and Ellis, who began to act immediately. Dana sought from federal district court judge Peleg Sprague a writ of *de homine replegiando*,* which would have freed Burns in his own recognizance. Sprague promptly denied the writ, charging that it was unknown in American law. Burns's counsel then went to the state courts where Daniel Wells, chief justice of the court of common pleas, did issue a writ of replevin** ordering Marshal Freeman to bring Burns before his court. Despite the fact that the writ treated Burns as chattel and was not based on the assumptions of habeas corpus, Marshal Freeman refused to surrender Burns to the sheriff who served the writ. At the same time that these manoeuvres were going on, Lewis Hayden, who had participated in the Shadrach rescue, filed a $10,000 damage suit against Suttle and Brent. Responding to his charge that they had conspired to have Burns arrested, the court demanded a $5,000 bail bond from each of them.

Within forty-eight hours of Burns's arrest, Bostonians had not only taken legal steps on his behalf, but were also contemplating extralegal action. "If this man is allowed to go back," Wendell Phillips's wife, Ann, wrote on May 25, "*there is no* anti slavery in Mass[achuset]ts—We may as well disband at

---

*A common law writ issued by a court to free a person under arrest on that individual's promise that he or she would appear at a specified time and place to answer any charges laid against him or her.

**A writ applied to goods and chattel which places them under bond until the issue of ownership between contesting parties has been established.

once if our meetings & papers are all talk & we never are to do any[thing] *but talk.*"[12] In this spirit the Boston Vigilance Committee met the next day and decided that whatever action they took to free Burns should occur at the courthouse the following morning when his hearing was scheduled to resume. Unsatisfied with so vague a commitment, some committee members, including Unitarian ministers Thomas Wentworth Higginson and Theodore Parker, abolitionist orator Wendell Phillips, and reformer Samuel Gridley Howe, planned to meet again that same evening in the anteroom of Faneuil Hall before the scheduled Burns rally took place.

Between the two meetings, events outran planning. Late that afternoon Martin Stowell, a principal organizer of the Jerry rescue now living in Worcester, arrived in Boston with some fifty supporters and soon convinced his minister, Higginson, that an attack on the courthouse should be made that night while the rally was in progress. Police attention, he argued, would then be focussed on Faneuil Hall and action at the courthouse would catch them off guard. In sum, Burns should be rescued before 10:30 P.M., when the meeting was expected to end and reinforcements might be anticipated at the courthouse.

Impetuous and eager for action, Higginson hurried to Faneuil Hall to present the new plan to his vigilance committee colleagues before the meeting got under way. By the time he got there, however, the crowds were already so dense and the noise so great that the plotters in the anteroom found it difficult even to hear each other. Ignoring the din, Higginson thought that he had made his plans clear to Howe and Parker and that Parker would, at some point, suddenly move an adjournment of the meeting and lead the crowd to the courthouse. Presumably also one of them would so inform Phillips, who was already on the stage. Alas for the rescue plan, Parker had not understood what Higginson had said, and no one undertook to tell Phillips about it. Consequently both of them gave their entire attention to the rally and to rousing its participants to be ready for action the next day.

Certainly if the Fugitive Slave Law was to be successfully thwarted on this occasion, solid public backing was indispensible. This was the rationale for the Faneuil Hall meeting. And the circumstances of the previous week led its sponsors to expect unusual enthusiasm. The day of the rally, the Senate had passed the final version of the Kansas-Nebraska bill by a 35-13 vote. The meeting's promotors pounced on the coincidence. The Free Soil *Commonwealth* announced, "Another Man Seized in Boston by the Man Hunters!! The Devil-Bill renewing its Vigor and getting up a Jubilee among us, on the passage of the Nebraska Bill."[13] And Boston generally responded in kind. Dana, whose antislavery activity had threatened his professional standing with local merchants and shipowners, marvelled at the change the Kansas-Nebraska bill had wrought. "The most remarkable exhibition is from the Whigs, the Hunker Whigs, the Compromise men of 1850. Men who would not speak to me in 1850 and 1851, and who enrolled themselves as special policemen in the Sims affair, stop me in the street and talk treason." "The Webster delusion," he concluded succinctly, "is passing off."[14] They were now openly opposing the Fugitive Slave Law.

It was indeed a remarkable phenomenon. Men so diverse as Cotton Whigs Edward Everett and Amos A. Lawrence on the one hand and Charles Sumner's supporters on the other were struck by the change, and they universally attributed it to the Kansas-Nebraska bill. Outside New England as well the change was noticed. The moderate Whig New York *Times* reported that former antiabolitionists were now petitioning for the Fugitive Slave Law's repeal; and the antislavery Whig *National Era* in Washington attributed Boston's violent response to the Burns affair directly to the "flagrant outrage" of the Kansas-Nebraska Act.[15] Among Northern radicals and conservatives alike, the repeal of the Missouri Compromise signalled a Southern rejection of compromise. Old Unionist assumptions were wrenched. As one of Sumner's correspondents put it, formerly conservative businessmen reacted to congressional action repealing "a part of the compromise measures" by demanding "now let us have them all repealed."[16]

The Rescue Attempt

Swarming out into the highly charged atmosphere of Boston, citizens thronged toward Faneuil Hall on the evening of May 26 and filled it to overflowing, waiting for the excitement the rally promised. They were not disappointed.

From the first, the speakers linked the day's events in Washington with Boston's concerns. Young John L. Swift announced the death of all compromises, "murdered by the Nebraska bill."[17] Then Samuel G. Howe offered a series of resolutions proclaiming "that as the South has decreed, in the late passage of the Nebraska bill, that no faith is to be kept with freedom; so, in the name of the living God, and on the part of the North, we declare that henceforth and forever no compromises should be made with Slavery."[18] To cap it all, Wendell Phillips tied the substance of the Kansas-Nebraska bill directly to the enforcement of the Fugitive Slave Law. "I am agains[t] squatter sovereignty in Nebraska," he proclaimed, "and against kidnappers' sovereignty in Boston." "Nebraska," he added, "I call knocking a man down, and this [Burns affair] is spitting in his face after he is down."[19]

If the mood was created by frustration with national politics, the substance of the meeting was more pointedly directed at preventing Burns's return to slavery. Thomas Sims, the crowd remembered, had been sent South after legal efforts failed to save him. The implication was clear. Legal aid was not enough. The assembly therefore adopted resolutions which not only challenged the law but barely stopped short of calling for revolution.

Resolved, That the time has come to declare and to demonstrate the fact that no slave-hunter can carry his prey from the Commonwealth of Massachusetts.

Resolved, That in the language of Algernon Sydney, "that which is not just is not law, and that which is not law ought not to be obeyed."

Resolved, That, leaving every man to determine for himself the mode of resistance, we are united in the glorious sentiment of our Revolutionary fathers—"Resistance to tyrants is obedience to God."[20]

The oratory to support them was even more fiery. Wendell Phillips, a man of considerable wealth, had given up his law practice some ten years earlier to work full time for reform. His popularity on the lecture circuit came from his manner as much as his substance for, in eschewing the formal rhetoric of the day, he seemed to speak so directly to each auditor that he held audiences spellbound for hours.

This evening Phillips's speech was brief and pointed. Boston's Mayor Smith had, he told his audience, forbidden the city police to assist federal officials in the Burns case as they had in the Sims case. Thus whether Burns was returned or not was in the hands of the people. Recently in other cities, and formerly in Boston, citizens had rescued fugitives from law officers and spirited them to freedom. Would Boston, he asked, "adhere to the result of the case of Shadrach or the case of Sims"? In conclusion, Phillips set the stage for a rescue attempt the next day. "See to it, every one of you, as you love the honor of Boston, that you watch this case so closely that you can look into that man's eyes. When he comes up for trial get a sight of him—and don't lose sight of him. There is nothing like the mute eloquence of a suffering man to urge to duty; be there, and I will trust the result."[21]

After Phillips finished, Theodore Parker took the rostrum. As well known in Boston and reform circles as Phillips, Parker was thought by some to be America's leading intellectual: a linguist, a philosopher, and a theologian. But he was as much at home on the platform as in his study, commanding as he did a liberal Unitarian congregation so large that he preached every Sunday from the stage of the great Boston Music Hall. He too knew how to reach and rouse his audience. Addressing the Faneuil Hall assembly as "fellow subjects" and "vassals of Virginia," he excoriated them for permitting the Fugitive Slave Law to operate in Boston. He reminded them that their very meeting place was the home of revolution, the seedbed for protests against the Stamp Act and Tea Act, against oppression and royal bondage. Now even Boston officialdom promised to stand aside if they should renew their revolutionary tradition in the Burns case. "Well, gentlemen," he concluded about the present after a long series of historical allusions, "I say there is one law—slave law; it is everywhere. There is another law, which also is a finality; and that law, it is in your hands and your arms, and you can put it in execution, just when you see fit." Although he was "a clergyman and a man of peace," he was not unwilling to mark out a course for direct action. "Now," he told the audience, "I am going to propose that when you adjourn, it be to meet at Court Square, to-morrow morning at nine o'clock"[22] (Document III-A-4).

But by this time there was already considerable confusion in the hall. Parker's speech had been interrupted several times; and when he made his call for action next morning voices from the rear of the hall cried out, "Let's go to-night."[23] Higginson's supporters were desperately trying to make up for their leader's failure to communicate. But no one on the stage except Howe had understood the new plan, and he had failed to explain it to the others, thinking they must already know. Higginson meanwhile had long since gone to Court Square to await the arrival of the crowd which he confidently expected. And Phillips, totally oblivious of Higginson's plan, spoke from the platform urging the crowd to hold off until morning. But the Higginson men in the back of the auditorium persisted. So, finally, leaderless and undirected, the crowd surged out of the hall, around the corner, and up the street to the courthouse, some four blocks away.

When those already at the courthouse heard the approaching crowd, they anticipated organized and efficient reinforcements and so began their attack. But the approaching crowd did little more than to alert the courthouse guards, who quickly bolted the outside doors against impending danger. Their action thwarted an assault on the east door of the building, led by Lewis Hayden, who even before the Shadrach rescue in Boston had participated in a successful rescue in Detroit. Momentarily stymied, Hayden led his followers to the west door at which point the crowd from Faneuil Hall began to arrive. Hoisting a battering ram, a dozen or more men, mostly black, charged repeatedly, smashing the timber against the door till it gave way. In an instant Higginson and one other man pushed through the broken door and entered the building. But no one followed them, and their expectation of sweeping past the defenders to rescue Burns was quickly dashed. Marshal Freeman and his deputies, including John Batchelder, a cartman with previous experience as a deputy during the Sims rendition, stood their ground. In the confusion of the repulse, Batchelder was killed, and Higginson cut on forehead and chin.

Alerted by the clamor, the city police rapidly appeared and began making arrests. Half of the first dozen persons taken into custody were black; among the whites arrested was Albert Browne, a Cambridge law student and son of a member of the Governor's Council. Meanwhile a group of four blacks and two whites led a second assault, charging through a basement door only to be caught in a cul-de-sac, where they vented their anger by smashing furniture until they were arrested. Among them was Martin Stowell, the Worcester man who had convinced Higginson to attack that night.

At roughly the same time and apparently quite by coincidence, the Boston artillery company, undergoing its monthly drill, heard the commotion and marched to Court Square to investigate. Before long Mayor J.V.C. Smith, desperate now to use all means to keep the peace, took advantage of the coincidence and ordered them, as well as the Columbian artillery company, to assist the police in restoring order and guarding the courthouse. Soon thereafter the square began to empty and by 12:30 A.M., less than three hours after the attack, it was deserted. Thus the affray ended. A handful of persons had been arrested; except for one battered door and numerous broken windows, the granite building stood as before; and Anthony Burns remained inside, still a prisoner.

The Unresolved Issues

In the immediate aftermath, those involved pondered the factors which had made the rescue attempt fail. Reviewing the whole Burns affair in a sermon two weeks later, Higginson contended that had only twenty more men bolstered the attack, they would have freed Burns. A report from a Cambridge man suggested how right he was. Allegedly, Marshal Freeman had confessed that his men were so frightened when Batchelder was killed that a mere "dozen resolute fellows" could easily have rushed the building and taken his prisoner.

To what extent, then, was the lack of manpower a result of Higginson's impetuosity? Certainly his Friday night coup destroyed the Parker-Phillips plan to rally forces for a showdown the next day and counteracted the action the Faneuil Hall meeting was intended to produce. Garrison, highly critical of the attack, wrote that it had "no connection whatever with the Faneuil Hall meeting, and was the act of some half dozen impulsive and unreasoning persons, without plan or system of any kind."[24] But then, what specific plans had the Vigilance Committee produced? Could the fiasco better be laid to irresponsibility on the part of Higginson, Stowell, and Hayden or to indecision in the Boston Vigilance Committee?

In the long run, however, the immediate factors which led to failure were less important than fundamental questions about the right to resist laws which a large portion of the community considered unjust. Commenting on May 27, the conservative Whig *Evening Transcript* of Boston asked, "What is our duty in this emergency? How far is the example of violating compacts to be followed?" Then it answered its own question. As long as the Fugitive Slave Law remained law, it said, all were obliged to obey it, "to join in no unlawful proceeding, or to countenance any measures which will not stand the test of the calmest reason, and be justified by our maturest reflection"[25] (Document III-D-2). Similarly the *Evening Journal*, though opposed to the law, reproached the rescuers for acting extralegally before they had exhausted all legal channels. "In their eagerness to trample upon the fugitive slave law," the *Journal* commented, "they forgot that inflammatory appeals and mob violence, instead of increasing the sympathy which every one felt for the unfortunate prisoner, would only arouse a feeling of indignation, and a deep settled determination among the law-abiding portion of the community to sustain the authorities in enforcing the laws."[26]

But could community interests legitimately sacrifice the freedom of individuals? What hope was there for people like Burns caught in the toils of this law? Did not simple humanity demand illegal action? Were not the actions proposed at the Faneuil Hall rally and applied by Higginson and his followers grounded in a moral necessity recognized by a law higher than human legislation? William Seward, who popularized the term "higher law," had early linked it to Christian obligation. Defending John Van Zandt, who had sheltered a fugitive in his Ohio home, Seward had held that Congress had "no power to interdict *any duty* enjoined by God on Mount Sinai, or inculcated by His Son, on the Mount of Olives."[27] Similarly, Parker, an increasingly frequent correspondent of Seward, argued the precedence of moral imperatives over statute law. Free Soilers like Joshua Giddings of Ohio and Charles Durkee of Wisconsin used similar arguments in justifying defiance of the Fugitive Slave Law. "It is a mistaken opinion . . . though honestly entertained by many," Durkee said at one point, "that crime becomes sanctified when committed in the name of law"[28] (Document III-C-1). And after the Burns rescue attempt, an obscure Massachusetts Baptist minister, E.H. Gray, reduced the question even more bluntly to one of individual conscience. "Then who shall decide when the laws of God and the laws of man conflict?" he added. "Each man for himself. . . . The State cannot decide that matter, the Church cannot, but every man must decide for himself, taking God's Word for his standard"[29] (Document III-C-2).

Many, however, feared that anarchy would result from so individualistic a following of the higher law. If every man lived by his private conscience, irrespective of community responsibility, government by men would replace government by impartial law. Judge John McLean of Ohio, sitting on a fugitive slave case in that state, had explicitly set aside his sympathies for the defendant as secondary to respect for law. "Sooner or later a disregard for the law could bring chaos, anarchy and wide-spread ruin," he said; "the law must be enforced."[30] Maine Senator James Bradbury was even more blunt. Directly challenging Wisconsin's Charles Durkee, he warned that "incalculable mischief, and even the destruction of everything in the form of government," would follow upon recourse to the higher law. Scorning those who would defy the law in the name of principle, he asked, "Does this law violate any of my personal rights as a citizen? Does it violate any of the personal rights of any citizen of a free State? Certainly not, except it be a personal right to resist the execution of any law we may not happen to like"[31] (Document III-D-1).

Bradbury's remarks suggested a freedom to decide which many advocates of the higher law denied on the grounds of religious obligation. Congregational clergyman Charles Beecher preached on the unequivocal "duty of disobedience to wicked laws."[32] And Samuel J. May taught his Syracuse congregation that Christians were morally bound not to return fugitives as they were morally bound not to steal or commit murder. His fellow Unitarian, John Weiss of Boston, writing in the wake of the Burns rendition, countered those who feared the anarchy which following the higher law implied. "The right of conscience in a law-abiding community does not lead to anarchy," he claimed. Social disruption comes only when evil laws are made which, by their oppressive nature, force men to disobey them. Humane law is then the only legitimate alternative to the threat of anarchy.[33]

Some of the participants in the rescue attempt were not so abstruse, and vindicated their actions in the name of revolution. Albert Browne wrote Higginson that "however others may look upon my conduct, I cannot but think that forcible, revolutionary resistance was justifiable."[34] Higginson fully sympathized. In his sermon, "Massachusetts in Mourning," preached the Sunday following the rendition, he argued that force was "sublime" when used in a "good cause." He despaired that change could be wrought through the legislative process, and confessed to his congregation, "I can only make life worth living for, by becoming a revolutionist"[35] (Document III-B-2).

If appeals to the higher law troubled many, open appeals to revolution appalled them. And revolutionary views were not confined to the actual rescuers, as Phillips's and Parker's speeches at Faneuil Hall attested. Even when analogies to the American revolution and eighteenth-century meetings in Boston's "cradle of liberty" suggested a desire to conserve old liberties rather than to establish new, the question arose whether any government, even one born in revolt, could tolerate calls for action challenging established law and the original governmental compact. The Washington *Star* may have been extreme in thinking the mob at the courthouse should have been gunned down; but in attributing its course to antislavery politicians like Giddings and Sumner, who encouraged violence by their "incendiary" and "traitorous appeals," it reflected Southern anxiety over unrestricted free speech. Nor was the unease confined to politics. In South Carolina the Charleston *Courier* found the behavior of the Faneuil Hall rally simple treason. The Mobile, Alabama, *Evening News* wanted to know why "the law pause[d] in this case? Why," it asked, "are not these traitors brought under its severest penalties? Hang a few of these madmen," the *News* concluded, "and the effect will be wholesome."[36] More moderately, the conservative New York *Journal of Commerce* wondered why "Theodore Parker, Wendell Phillips and other insurrectionist leaders [were not] taken into custody at the moment that their speeches gave the first occasion to the riot?"[37]

Thus the debate which raged about the fact and theory of the rescue attempt dealt with basic social and political questions. When, if ever, are citizens justified in breaking laws they believe to be unjust? Can violence ever be a legitimate social remedy? Can society allow the moral conviction of a few to set at naught the governmental and legal processes of the many? Should men be punished for their speech as well as their action? Pragmatically, the recourse to violence in the Burns affair failed of its object. But what if it had succeeded? Would that have changed any of the arguments?

Notes

1. James D. Richardson, comp., *A Compilation of the Messages and Papers of the Presidents*. . . (New York: Bureau of National Literature, 1897-1917), 6:2735.

2. Allen Nevins, *Ordeal of the Union* (New York: Charles Scribner, 1947), 2:43.

3. Roy Nichols, *Franklin Pierce: Young Hickory of the Granite Hills*, rev. ed. (Philadelphia: University of Pennsylvania Press, 1958), 300-01.

4. Albany *Evening Journal*, n.d., reprinted in *Frederick Douglass' Paper*, March 4, 1853.

5. Quoted in Claude M. Fuess, *The Life of Caleb Cushing* (New York: Harcourt, Brace and Co., 1923), 2:139-40.

6. Caleb Cushing to Franklin Pierce, November 14, 1853, in C.C. Andrews, ed., *Official Opinions of the Attorneys General of the United States* (Washington: Robert Farnham, 1856), 6:222.

7. U.S., Congress, Senate, *Congressional Globe*, 31st Cong., 2nd sess., February 22, 1851, Appendix, 310.

8. *Ibid.*, 32nd Cong., 1st sess., August 26, 1852, Appendix, 1112.

9. *Ibid.*, 32nd Cong., 1st sess., August 26, 1852, Appendix, 1117.

10. Amos A. Lawrence to William Appleton, March 6, 1854, Letterpress; A.A. Lawrence Papers, Massachusetts Historical Society.

11. Dana's diary, May 25, 1854; in Charles Francis Adams, *Richard Henry Dana: A Biography* (1890; Detroit: Gale Research, 1968), 1:265.

12. Ann G. Phillips to Anne and Deborah Weston, [May 25, 1854]; Antislavery Collection, Boston Public Library.

13. *The Boston Slave Riot, and Trial of Anthony Burns.* . . (Boston: Fetridge and Company, 1854), 19.

14. Dana, diary, May 26, 1854, in Adams, *Dana*, 1:269-70.

15. *National Era*, June 1, 1854.

16. John W. Sullivan to Charles Sumner, May 30, 1854; Sumner Papers, Houghton Library, Harvard University.

17. *Boston Journal*, n.d., reprinted in New York *Daily Tribune*, May 29, 1854.

18. *Ibid.*

19. *Boston Slave Riot*, 9.

20. Boston *Journal*, n.d., reprinted in New York *Daily Tribune*, May 29, 1854.

21. *Ibid.*

22. Theodore Parker, *The Trial of Theodore Parker.* . . (Boston: The Author, 1855), 199-203.

23. *Ibid.*, 203.

24. *Liberator*, June 2, 1854.

25. Boston *Evening Transcript*, May 27, 1854.

26. Boston *Evening Journal*, May 27, 1854, reprinted in New York *Daily Times*, May 29, 1854.

27. William Henry Seward, *In the Supreme Court of the United States. John Van Zandt, ad sectum Wharton Jones. Argument for the Defendant* (Albany: Weed, Parsons & Co., 1847), 39.

28. U.S., Congress, House, *Congressional Globe*, 32nd Cong., 1st sess., August 6, 1852, Appendix, 887.

29. E.H. Gray, *Assaults Upon Freedom! or, Kidnapping an Outrage upon Humanity and Abhorrent to God. A Discourse, Occasioned by the Rendition of Anthony Burns* (Shelburne Falls, Mass.: D.B. Gunn, 1854), 14.

30. Miller v. McQuerry, 5 McLean 469 (1853), quoted in Stanley W. Campbell, *The Slave Catchers: Enforcement of the Fugitive Slave Law, 1850-1860* (Chapel Hill: University of North Carolina Press, 1970), 122.

31. U.S., Congress, Senate, *Congressional Globe*, 32nd Cong., 1st sess., August 26, 1852, Appendix, 1123.

32. Charles Beecher, *The Duty of Disobedience to Wicked Laws. A Sermon on the Fugitive Slave Law* (New York: John A. Gray, 1851).

33. John Weiss, *Reform and Repeal. . .and Legal Anarchy.* . . (Boston: Crosby, Nichols & Co., 1854), 23-30.

34. Albert G. Browne, jr., to Thomas W. Higginson, June 19, [1854], in Thomas W. Higginson, comp., Ms Correspondence, etc., Relating to the Anthony Burns Episode, etc., 1851-1900. Antislavery Collection, Boston Public Library.

35. Thomas W. Higginson, *Massachusetts in Mourning.* . . (Boston: James Munroe & Co., 1854), 13.

36. Mobile, Alabama, *Evening News*, n.d., reprinted in Charleston, S.C., *Courier*, June 10, 1854.

37. New York *Journal of Commerce*, n.d., reprinted in *Liberator*, June 9, 1854.

4

The Rendition of Anthony Burns

The failure of the rescue attempt returned initiative in the Burns case to duly constituted authority: to the courts and to the local, state, and national executives responsible for administering the law. But it also set a new context for their actions. Was it now even more mandatory for the Pierce administration to make it an all-out test of the judicial machinery's ability and, if necessary, the military's power to enforce the law? Or, in view of the fervid local opposition, sparked by congressional repeal of old compromises, should the federal government avoid a head-on collision? Both sides showed caution. Some who had earlier advised full compliance with the law and who heartily disapproved both Phillips's and Parker's revolutionary appeals as well as the courthouse attack now counselled accommodation. Others who had long opposed enforcement of the fugitive law and had consciously thwarted it concluded, on simple humanitarian grounds, that a mutually agreeable resolution of the impasse was preferable. Early on Saturday morning the issue seemed to hang on the course of the hearing.

At nine o'clock the principals met with Commissioner Loring in the federal district court room of the courthouse. Immediately Suttle's junior counsel, Edward G. Parker, urged swift action, citing the preceding evening's disturbances. Burns's junior counsel, Charles M. Ellis, objected and was almost immediately seconded by senior counsel Dana, who, having just arrived, took charge from his associate. The defense, he argued, needed still more time to prepare its case. It was less than three days since Burns had been arrested on a false robbery charge, been hurried to the courthouse, and there been intimidated by his alleged master.

Undue haste and concealment on the part of federal officials was suggested when, the following morning, Burns had been brought before Commissioner Loring a full hour before the usual opening of court. It was true that at that time Loring had granted a delay until Saturday. But, Dana pointed out, the commissioner's intention to allow reasonable time for Burns to decide on counsel and for counsel to prepare had been frustrated by Marshal Freeman. When Burns's employer, Coffin Pitts, and his pastor, Leonard Grimes, sought to advise the prisoner and get his decision, the marshal had refused them access until they appealed to Dana, who interceded with the commissioner, who then forced the marshal to reverse himself. As a result of this delay, Dana and Ellis had had barely twenty-four hours to work on the case before the present hearing.

Seth M. Thomas, the claimant's senior counsel, already well-experienced in such cases by having acted the same role in the Shadrach and Sims cases, protested Dana's request. Under the 1850 law, he contended, the hearing was an administrative, not a judicial procedure. His client had all the documentation the law required to show that Burns was both his slave and a fugitive; and, in addition, Burns had corroborated these claims before witnesses. Under the circumstances the commissioner had no alternative but to fulfill his administrative obligation, and issue Suttle a certificate for Burns's return to Virginia.

A man of moderate temper and open mind, Loring was not pressed by Thomas's insistence. Before he became involved in this case, he had been respected by reformers, even abolitionists, for his charitable activities as well as for his legal prowess. As judge and teacher he was accustomed to exploring all sides. Now, facing both Dana and Thomas, Loring upheld this reputation. Taking account of both their arguments, he once again postponed the hearing to insure the defense its legal privileges. Until it was proved otherwise, Loring argued, Burns must be considered a freeman and his rights respected. For him to enjoy those rights, his counsel needed adequate time to prepare their briefs. External matters and "the excitement of the community,"[1] Loring concluded, could have no bearing on his decision. He then adjourned the hearing until eleven o'clock Monday morning.

The Purchase Attempt

The time thus bought was well used. All day Saturday Leonard Grimes sought funds to purchase Burns's freedom and thus legally to short-circuit the fugitive law. Significantly, Grimes, respected by both blacks and whites, went not to an abolitionist but to Hamilton Willis, a State Street broker, for assistance in drawing up the subscription document, which he then circulated among Boston's leading citizens.

The difficulties which Grimes encountered, as well as his ultimate success in raising the $1,200 for which Suttle had agreed to sell Burns, testify to the intense public interest stirred up by the case. For many, there was a real crisis of conscience. Abbott Lawrence, long known as a Cotton Whig, refused Grimes's request lest his action give consent to the enforcement of the Fugitive Slave Law. Others refused on the grounds that to contribute would attest to the law's unenforcibility in Boston. Yet some of similar opinion, like Samuel Eliot, who as a congressman had voted for the fugitive slave bill in 1850, did help Grimes. Of the donors, some were motivated by simple humanitarianism; others by a desire to thwart the fugitive law; still others hoped merely to avoid further mob violence and disruption, and pledged their money only if the sale were completed before the hearing resumed.

By eight o'clock that evening Grimes still lacked almost half the purchase price. Then not only Willis but even Suttle's lawyers came to his assistance. Willis advanced the difference between the $665 for which Grimes had obtained pledges and $800, while Parker and Thomas raised the remaining $400. Then at eleven o'clock Grimes, Parker, Thomas, and Willis met in Commissioner Loring's office where the latter prepared the legal papers necessary for the sale. When his attorneys announced that Suttle would take only cash, Willis, prepared for such a contingency, left to get the money. Shortly thereafter the group reassembled in Marshal Freeman's office for the final transaction. There they were joined by federal district attorney, Benjamin F. Hallett.

Hallett's presence doomed the sale. He came not simply as the government's attorney but as the agent of an administration determined that in this case nothing must abort its efforts to satisfy the slaveholding South by successfully enforcing the law. As soon as the group reassembled, Hallett commenced delaying actions designed to block the sale. During the day he had already established his tack when he convinced one potential donor to withdraw his offer, assuring him "that the slave could not be purchased,—that he must be tried."[2] Now he raised one objection after another until the clock should strike midnight, when the state's blue laws would compel delaying the business transaction until Monday morning. Striving to negate the lure of cash in hand, he implied a much larger loss to Suttle should he sell Burns at this juncture, for the federal government would, in such circumstances, probably not bear the extensive enforcement costs already incurred on his behalf. Moreover, he insisted that the sale could not be completed unless Suttle were personally present—which he was not. And even if the sale were concluded, he added, it would be illegal because Massachusetts law forbade the buying and selling of slaves within the state. Time passed while he spun out his arguments—and then it was midnight. Grasping his victory, Hallett announced that the proceedings could no longer continue. Nothing more could be done until Monday, and so the meeting broke up.

Hallett's manoeuvre paid off, for in the forced interim Suttle reconsidered the matter. On Monday morning, when Willis tried to complete the purchase, the Virginian announced his change of mind. He insisted to Willis that he had agreed to sell only if the transaction was concluded on Saturday. But his counsel, Edward Parker, noted that external pressures had been brought to bear on his client. "The claimant being advised thereto by many lovers of law and order, declines to negotiate further until it is first established that the supremacy of the law can be maintained."[3]

Thus the issue was joined. Until Monday morning it seemed possible to avoid a clear-cut showdown. As fugitive slave law commissioner, Judge Loring had carefully protected Burns's legal rights, and, on his own, had assisted the purchase attempt by staying late in his office on Saturday night to draw up the requisite legal documents. Parker, Suttle's counsel, had convinced the Virginian to sell his slave. And State Street merchants and brokers, who on Monday, frustrated by Hallett's manoeuvres, would organize a massive petition for the repeal of the fugitive law, had on Saturday offered contributions to Grimes.

Yet Hallett's behavior and Suttle's change of mind suggest, by contrast, that the federal government did seek a showdown. In the face of persistent efforts by Hamilton Willis to purchase Burns with funds subscribed not by abolitionists but by Boston's "most respectable citizens," Suttle refused to budge, turning down at one point an offer of $4,000. Beyond question, pressure was brought on him by his Virginia neighbors. They doubtless feared that if Burns were bought free rather than sent home, their slaves would assume that any fugitive who was caught in the North would be similarly treated—and would act accordingly.

And at least equally decisive was the pressure which Hallett exerted on Suttle. Though following a course marked out by President Pierce and Attorney General Cushing, the district attorney was not a simple pawn. Having begun his career in the 1830s as an editor of a reform newspaper, tolerant if not sympathetic to Garrisonian abolitionism, Hallett had since become a conservative Democrat and a professional politician. In addition to having edited the Boston *Post*, he had held a series of patronage posts, including that of fugitive slave commissioner, and in 1852 had served as chairman of the Democratic National Committee. A man with power as well as the agent of administration policy, Hallett was a man to impress a small-time Virginia politician and shopkeeper. When the district attorney reminded him that somebody would have to pay for the 100 federal troops already called out to keep the peace, he undoubtedly terrified Suttle, who knew the law's requirement that a losing claimant must pay all the legal costs. No wonder the Virginian fell in with the government's plan.

The Presence of Federal Troops

The use of troops illustrated just how hard a line the federal government had drawn. No sooner had the rescue attempt failed than Marshal Freeman sent his deputy to East Boston to charter a steamboat and bring in troops from Fort Independence to guard the courthouse. And even before they could arrive, a force of marines from the Boston Navy yard took up stations at the courthouse. Acting with alacrity and perhaps recalling his chastisement for inefficiency in such matters, Freeman then telegraphed President Pierce, and informed him that he had availed himself "of the resources of the United States" "in consequence of an attack upon the Court House."[4] With equal speed the president replied in a widely publicized telegram: "Your conduct is approved. The law must be enforced."[5]

Freeman had acted under a War and Navy Department policy, established in 1851, which authorized federal marshals to use troops in an emergency. Nevertheless, there was some question about the legality of his actions. Federal troops had been summoned after the Christiana rescue in 1851, but only to restore order and keep the peace. In the Burns case, however, there had been no rescue. The function of the troops was clearly that of assisting officials in carrying out the Fugitive Slave Law. The question of using troops in this capacity had already been raised, when, after the Shadrach rescue, President Fillmore had sought a change in 1795 law requiring the president to issue a warning proclamation before he could call the state militia into national service in the case of insurgency. The Congress had rejected his request. In the present crisis Pierce raised a similar question: could justice department officials call for troops to enforce the Fugitive Slave Law of 1850? In response, on Saturday morning, in the wake of the Faneuil Hall meeting and the attempted rescue, Attorney General Cushing hastily wrote an opinion justifying the use both of federal troops and state militia. The law provided, he argued, that a posse comitatus could be drafted into action by a federal marshal for its enforcement. Like all other adult males, militiamen and federal troops were subject to a posse comitatus call. That they happened also to constitute a military unit was incidental—though it was clearly useful. To clinch his argument, Cushing found that the 1852 statute providing that extraordinary expenses incurred in carrying out a federal law be born by the government, justified federal payment of regulars and militia while they served in this capacity. Thus Marshal Freeman's use of both federal and state troops, should he need them, was both just and proper (Document II-B-2).

With these added powers of enforcement, government officials awaited the resumption of the Burns hearing. On Monday morning, May 29, 100 federal troops and a civilian posse of 100 armed citizens guarded the courthouse, which was cordoned off by heavy ropes. Their presence was not altogether welcome. As soon as the hearing began, defense counsel Ellis protested the military atmosphere and the indignity to counsel which it produced. He and Dana had both "been stopped [by the troops] and grossly annoyed on their way"[6] to the hearing. Then pressing his point, he moved a change of venue.* But District Attorney Hallett, whose presence in court was as gratuitous as it had been at the purchase negotiations, forced his counterargument on the commissioner. Ignoring Loring's attempt to call him to order, Hallett persisted. "The guards," he said, "had been set and all the objectionable appearances were required to prevent the destruction of the building and secure the safety of the Court in the excited state of feeling created by the counsel and action of the gentleman (Ellis) and his friends."[7] The troops, he continued, were part of a legal posse—sanctioned by the president of the United States himself.

But the building thus defended was not a federal building. Municipally owned, it housed primarily state courts. The federal court merely leased its quarters. Not only Burns's counsel, therefore, objected to the dominating presence of federal troops. Some state supreme court justices threatened to cancel their sessions, especially after an inferior court judge had been held at bayonet point. That the protests were not an antislavery bugbear was born out by those who sympathized with Suttle. A young Harvard student from Georgia wrote that "the room is filled with armed men; even the counsel at bar have their revolvers and bowie knives."[8] Counsel Parker, admitting he was

*A change of the place in which trial is held, usually because of circumstances militating against a fair trial in the original venue.

armed, observed, "Boston is a Barrack. The Court House is a Camp."[9] But it was Horace Greeley of the New York *Tribune* who best summed up the implications for Burns. "There is folly in opposing unarmed men to men with their pockets full of revolvers, and their belts gleaming with sabers. It is equally inexpedient to oppose artillery with pistols."[10]

Yet those who justified the armed presence had a strong case. The rhetoric of Faneuil Hall and the attack on the courthouse had dramatically demonstrated the lengths to which the law's opponents were willing to go. Already one law officer had been killed. And, even after the Friday night tragedy, threats of violence persisted. A mob of 500 to 1,000 persons, largely black, milled about the courthouse all day Saturday, increased, at one point, by a delegation of 400 from New Bedford. By ten o'clock in the evening an estimated 2,500 persons filled Court Square, apparently held in check only by the hastily strung cordon and several militia units. Though actual violence was minimal, at least a dozen persons were arrested in various disturbances. Late that evening, after the purchase attempt had failed, Hallett's carriage was followed and stopped by a group of blacks, who dispersed only when police approached.

The threat of violence was very real. On Sunday placards announced the failure of the purchase attempt and urged, "Be on your guard against all lies. Watch the slave pen. Let every man attend the trial."[11] On Monday morning, while the hearing was in session, 200 members of the Worcester Freedom Club appeared. Marching two by two they entered Court Square, made a show of strength, turned about and retired to Tremont Temple where, said the New York *Times*, they heard "inflammatory addresses" from Garrison and other antislavery leaders. Then they sought volunteers "to aid one of the Boston Coroners who was willing to serve a writ of *replevin* or *habeas corpus*, to take the fugitive BURNS from the United States Marshal."[12] Later in the day, as many as 7,000 persons were reported to be crowding into Court Square. Amos A. Lawrence, who described the impact of the Burns crisis on respectable Boston, caught the city's temper. "We went to bed one night old fashioned, conservative, Compromise Union Whigs & waked up stark mad Abolitionists."[13] He expected that "the people will prevail, but there will be bloodshed almost certainly."[14] As the vigil of Burns supporters at the courthouse continued throughout the following week, tensions remained high.

The Role of City and State Governments

The Friday night rescue attempt, the danger of similar disturbances, the various incidents, and the crowds which milled unceasingly in front of the courthouse sucked both city and state government into the crisis. J.V.C. Smith, a physician and amateur sculptor, had been relatively unknown when he had entered local politics as a Know-Nothing, and, despite his inexperience and a vacillating character, been elected mayor of the city. Peculiarly, his nativist, anti-Catholic political affiliation did little to disrupt his close business and personal ties with Irish Catholics, including Bishop John B. Fitzpatrick. His main support had come from the Lawrences and other Cotton Whigs who shaped the local Know-Nothing party into a moderately conservative replacement for the declining Whigs. Smith, undoubtedly shocked, as were his backers, by the Nebraska Act, had initially sympathized with the Faneuil Hall meeting. Thus, also, he had publicly pledged that municipal police would not help enforce the Fugitive Slave Law.

At the same time, however, the mayor was responsible for the city's peace. Faced with mobs, riot, and murder, he was caught amid conflicting pressures. Amos Lawrence tried to hold him to the course he first charted, writing that "the citizens & the conservative portion of them w[oul]d prefer to see the Courthouse razed, rather than that the fugitive now confined there sh[oul]d be returned to slavery."[15] But the advice came after Smith had already changed course. As soon as the rescue attempt was made, he ordered two militia companies on duty to restore and keep order. The next morning he addressed the crowd assembled in Court Square, urging them to disperse. Later in the day, he issued a proclamation which, in requesting "peace and good order," concluded, "The laws must be obeyed, let the consequences be what they may."[16]

Spurned by the mayor, Burns's supporters turned to the Whig governor, Emory Washburn. He might, they hoped, use the militia to other purposes, ordering it to serve Marshal Freeman with the writ of replevin which he had refused to accept from the sheriff. Washburn, however, turned them down (Document IV-A-1). Believing neither that the Fugitive Slave Law was unconstitutional nor that the marshal had acted illegally, he saw no reason to accede to their request. Furthermore, he doubted the governor's power to order the militia out except in direct response to threatened or actual violence. Even more discouraging to Burns's supporters was his positive conception of the militia's role in times of civil disturbance. Addressing the Independent Cadets three days after he had turned the abolitionists' request down, he assessed the municipal police force as too weak to cope with crises like the present one. The only competent civic resource available to handle emergencies and maintain public order under stress was the militia, which he implied were used correctly in the days following the rescue attempt. To have committed them to serve one of the interested parties would have destroyed their utility as a law and order force.

In so saying, Governor Washburn supported Mayor Smith. Boston's aldermen, however, did not. On Monday they met and voted unanimously that the mayor should dismiss the militia he had ordered out. The mayor refused, claiming he was solely responsible for the city's defense. Frustrated, one of the aldermen complained to Sumner that "our Mayor has deceived us all.... Instead of advising with his Aldermen he went for counsel to Hallett—Freeman & Isaac H. Wright [one of the militia commanders]. What pitiable weakness."[17] Defeated once, the aldermen then discussed instructing Smith to evict the marines from the courthouse and to forbid federal officials using it as a jail for fugitive slaves. The mayor's own vote was needed to defeat the plan.

It is probable that throughout Mayor Smith was pressed hard by Washington to keep the militia on duty. Pierce had authorized Hallett to "incur any expense deemed necessary by the Marshal and yourself, for city military or otherwise, to insure the execution of the law."[18] But in the circumstances, Smith welcomed the federal subvention of the militia, which enabled him more readily to do his duty as mayor, maintaining law and order in the city (Document IV-B-1). In any case he ignored abolitionist protests that he was violating the 1843 Massachusetts law forbidding state and local office holders to assist in returning fugitives. The mayor could well argue that his actions were within the purview of keeping the peace; that the militia was not being used to return Anthony Burns to slavery or to enforce the Fugitive Slave Law, but only to forestall violence. To his opponents, however, action to prevent a rescue meant de facto assistance in enforcing the 1850 statute.

The Legal Arguments

While these questions were publicly debated, the hearing, which resumed on Monday morning, continued for three days. Even admission to the courtroom became an issue, with the New York *Tribune* reporting that entry tickets were issued only to government supporters; truckers and others of the "right" sort. Apparently too, Samuel May, Jr., general agent of the American Anti-Slavery Society, was excluded even though he had managed to obtain a pass. But the exclusion of abolitionists was not absolute, for Ohio congressman Joshua Giddings, in town for a Free Soil convention, Wendell Phillips, and Theodore Parker all attended the hearing.

Responding to the threatening presence of troops and the hostile courthouse atmosphere, Dana continued to protest their influence on the hearing. Judges and lawyers were, he charged, continually harassed by drunken soldiers and the one-quarter of the marshal's posse who had previously served time in jail. The result was not only a sordid atmosphere but one prejudicial to Burns. His associate Ellis went still further, charging that the hearing had become a political ploy. How else could Hallett's intervention be explained; and how else the strange coincidence of Burns's arrest with the passage of the Kansas-Nebraska bill? He could only conclude "that there are influences at work, which make this anything but a trial."[19]

Neither of Burns's counsel, however, confined himself to protest. The major arguments of both ranged from matters of legal form to basic constitutional issues. First they raised the technical issues. The proffered proof of Burns's identity was so vague that it presented strong likelihood of mistaken identity. Furthermore the testimony adduced to prove that an Anthony Burns was Suttle's slave was insufficient, being merely transcripts rather than notarized true copies. Even if they were taken at face value, their substance did not establish slave status beyond doubt. Finally the defense contended that both the complaint and the warrant for Burns's arrest were improperly drawn and that therefore the hearing itself was invalid.

Turning then to substantive questions, Dana and Ellis contended that Burns's conversation with Suttle immediately after his arrest was inadmissable as evidence. First of all, it was involuntary testimony from a much intimidated prisoner. Secondly, the 1850 statute specifically excluded testimony from an alleged fugitive. Here, although Commissioner Loring was perplexed, he admitted Burns's testimony, but indicated he might later reconsider. Forced then to respond to the confession, counsel claimed that Burns's statements, taken as a whole, proved he was not a fugitive as defined by law, for the confession maintained that he had fallen asleep while loading a vessel and had inadvertently been brought to Boston. Thus there was no conscious choice to flee service. Finally, they introduced witnesses who testified that at the date the complaint set for Burns's escape from Virginia, he was already in Boston and employed as a window washer at the Mattapan Iron Works.

At the very last, Burns's lawyers spoke to the question of the Fugitive Slave Law's constitutionality. It prohibited trial by jury and circumvented the right of habeas corpus. It offered no protection against unreasonable seizure. And it not only violated individual rights but states' rights in decreeing that a deposition of the slave's identity from the court in one state be binding on the courts in another.

Seth Thomas, in his closing statement, rebutted some of the defense but argued that most of it was simply irrelevant. The Fugitive Slave Law was clear in language and meaning and fully constitutional. Thus there was no point in arguing about it. The evidence which the claimant presented fully met its two requirements for the return of a slave. The Virginia court record stating that Anthony Burns owed service to Charles Suttle was sufficient to establish that fact. And, secondly, the slave described in that document was clearly the same Burns who was in the courtroom. After raising questions about the reliability of the testimony that Burns was in Boston prior to the time the complaint said he had escaped, Thomas concluded that the exact time of escape was irrelevant. All that the law required was evidence that Burns did owe service, that he had escaped, and that the present prisoner was, in fact, the Burns alluded to. All these requirements the claimant had met.

On Wednesday afternoon, with the arguments on both sides completed, the commissioner recessed the proceedings until Friday, June 2, at which time he promised his decision. Punctually at nine o'clock Friday morning, Edward Loring entered the courtroom and read that decision. After a lengthy weighing of the evidence and arguments presented by both sides, it ruled in favor of Charles Suttle. Anthony Burns was Suttle's slave, he had escaped from service, and he must, therefore, be returned to his master in Virginia. Abolitionists were appalled by Loring's narrow line of argument. He ruled flatly that there was no reason to question the Fugitive Slave Law's constitutionality. The role in which it cast the commissioner was purely administrative, not judicial; a question merely of extradition no different for fugitives from service than for fugitives from justice (Document II-A-3). Therefore the law's failure to require a jury trial to establish the fugitive's identity was quite correct. Consequently there was no alternative but to rule for the claimant.

The Triumph of Law and Order

Both city and federal officials were prepared for Loring's decision. District Attorney Hallett and Marshal Freeman had made full plans for Burns's rendition South, which Washington had approved. Doubtless correct in their denial of previous knowledge of the decision, they had begun early in the week to assemble forces sufficient to carry out the ruling they expected. On Tuesday evening, another contingent of marines arrived in the city from Portsmouth, New Hampshire. Alongside a wharf the chartered steamer *John Taylor* stood ready to carry Burns to the revenue cutter *Morris* lying out in the harbor. On Wednesday Secretary of War Davis had ordered the adjutant general to go to Boston and, after conferring with the marshal and district attorney, to call up additional federal troops if they were needed. Davis, who three years earlier had, as a senator, thought that "the ends of the public justice [would] be better subserved and the laws better maintained without any attempt to overawe the public by a resort to military force,"[20] now, as a cabinet member, reflected the Pierce administration's hard line.

Mayor Smith and the city government were similarly ready to rely on the military. Marshal Freeman, seconded by Hallett, had warned the mayor on Tuesday that the police and city militia then on duty could not keep the peace if trouble broke out and had pressed him to call up additional militia units. In different times the mayor might well have asked **why** federal officials were advising him how to run the city, or have protested being pressured to violate state law by assisting in the rendition of a slave. But the matter was presented as a matter of cooperation, the federal officials insisting that they were not calling upon him to aid in enforcing the "*fugitive law* as such" but only to see to the preservation of the peace of the city and the suppression of organized rebellion. They also played on Smith's fears of a situation developing which he could not handle. "If bloodshed is to be prevented in the public streets, there must be such a demonstration of a military force as will overawe attack, and avoid an inevitable conflict between the armed posse of the Marshal and the rioters."[21] The mayor, fully impressed, followed their suggestions even to the point of putting the city under martial law on the day of the rendition. And finally, the president's assurances that the federal treasury would bear the costs got through to the mayor. He agreed to the suggestions of the federal officials for the day of the rendition as he had agreed to earlier ones and pledged to "preserve the peace with all the military and police of the city."[22]

The legality of the mayor's action was open to real question (Document IV-B-2). Despite Hallett's assurances that city forces would not be used to enforce the Fugitive Slave Law, the only justification for the federal government's paying their expenses was Attorney General Cushing's ruling that military forces could be drafted as part of the marshal's posse for which the 1850 law provided. The payment of federal funds for the city militia and police clearly indicated that from Washington's view at least they were enforcing the Fugitive Slave Law and were thus violating the Massachusetts law of 1843 which prohibited their use for that purpose. Four Boston aldermen protested the legality of the mayor's actions on the grounds that they were taken without the consent and against the advice of the Board of Aldermen.

Nonetheless, as soon as Loring announced his decision on June 2, Mayor Smith proclaimed martial law and gave to Major General J. Cushing Edmands, commander of the First Division of Massachusetts Volunteer Militia and Police Chief Robert Taylor "full discretionary power to sustain the laws of the land."[23] Although one police captain immediately resigned his job rather than execute "that infamous 'Fugitive Slave Bill,' "[24] the rest obeyed orders and, with the militia, cleared and lined the streets which Burns would traverse from the courthouse to the wharves. At half-past two in the afternoon, Anthony Burns went down that route accompanied by one of the most formidable escorts a slave ever had. Leading the procession was a detachment from the National Boston Lancers. After them came a company of United States infantry. They were followed by a company of marines. Next came Burns, inside a hollow square composed of sixty volunteer guards and flanked by another company of marines. At the rear followed a six-pound cannon, loaded and ready for use, and a final company of marines.

Whether so large a force was necessary is moot. There was no rescue attempt; but there were incidents. A bottle of vitriol and some red pepper were tossed at the marching men from a window in the building on State Street occupied by the *Commonwealth*, but they harmed no one. A cartman who tried to cross the militia line lost his horse to their bayonets, and someone in the crowd stabbed the horse of one of the soldiers. When the crowd pressed forward in curiosity, a frightened militia captain ordered his men to open fire, but an alert superior instantly countermanded the order. Elsewhere along the line of march at least two other civilians were injured, and federal troops were the targets of stones and bricks. But no major violence occurred. Even a last minute change of route as the procession approached the wharves triggered no concerted attempt to disrupt the proceedings. Soon Anthony Burns was taken aboard the *John Taylor*, in the slip at T wharf, and transported to his waiting master aboard the *Morris*, which lay at anchor "in the stream." The rendition was complete.

Federal officials, particularly Hallett and Freeman, were satisfied with a job well done. The Boston correspondent of the Charleston, South Carolina, *Courier* was sure that "the abolitionists [had been] ripe for murder, and [that] nothing but a display of the military dismayed them."[25] Both the large numbers of Bostonians and out-of-towners who lined the streets and private correspondence among abolitionists suggest he may well have been right. But the district attorney and the marshal knew their obligations and had met them. They had prevented riot, enforced the law, and returned Burns.

The role which Mayor Smith played, however, is more complex and difficult to assess. Had he, in his use of militia and police, enforced one law only to violate another? Had he simply met his duty as mayor to preserve the city's peace; or, in accepting federal funds to pay for that action, had he violated the 1843 state law? Had he any choice? With his aldermen against him, where else could he have turned for the funds needed by carry out his mayoral obligations? On the other hand, by acting as he did, had he followed his own "higher law" and transgressed his legal authority? Or did the extraordinary circumstances of a city swarming with crowds openly hostile to the enforcement of the Fugitive Slave Law justify extraordinary precautionary actions? Damned by abolitionists, Mayor Smith won commendation from those who put law and order first. Yet in the next city canvass he failed to be reelected.

More problematic than the dispute which surrounded the mayor's actions was the wisdom of using military force to enforce civil law. Did it increase or decrease both respect for law and the likelihood of domestic tranquility? New Hampshire's John Hale thought that Washington's reliance on federal troops betrayed a distrust of state government's will and ability to enforce the law, which in the end only undercut local authority. The Pensacola, Florida, *Gazette*, concerned about America's international standing, worried lest the episode expose the nation's inability, short of extreme measures, to "quell a mob of three thousand fanatics."[26] Others, like the New York *Journal of Commerce*, thought federal force increased rather than eroded respect for law, and praised the government's triumph "over one of the most ferocious gangs of Abolitionists, black and white, clerical and laical, that ever disgraced the country."[27]

Whether from strength or weakness, Washington also sought to punish those who had tried to thwart the law. Actually the first round of legal action occurred in Boston's municipal court. Those arrested in the courthouse fracas were initially held without bail on charges of felonious assault and murder. But even this action was designed primarily to ease the impact of enforcing the Fugitive Slave Law, since only four days after Burns's rendition the charges were reduced and the prisoners freed on bail. Of the eighteen originally arrested five were now charged only with riot and disturbance of the peace, and four with manslaughter. The remaining nine were released. Two of those charged with riot immediately pled guilty; and, when the municipal grand jury refused to indict all the rest except for riot, those earlier charged with manslaughter also pled guilty to the lesser charge. In the end, none of those men who refused to plead guilty were convicted.

The Pierce administration was dissatisfied with the municipal court's action, and therefore opened federal prosecution. In December 1854 seven of those originally arrested and seven others, including Higginson, Parker, and Phillips, were indicted by a federal grand jury, significantly not for violating the Fugitive Slave Act of 1850 or even that of 1793, but for disobeying a 1790 federal statute prohibiting willful obstruction, resistance, and opposition to a federal officer serving or executing a federal writ or process. The trial in the circuit court lasted only one day. On April 3, when defense challenges to the indictments had been heard, Judge Peleg Sprague squashed the indictment of the first defendant, Martin Stowell. He acted on the narrowest of the many legal objections offered by defense counsel, that the indictment did "not allege and set forth fully and sufficiently the authority and the proceedings whereon the alleged warrant and order [for Burns's arrest] were based."[28] Seeing that the objection held as well for all the others on trial, District Attorney Hallett avoided total defeat by moving simply to drop prosecution of all charges. Against defense protests, the judge so ordered and the case was closed. Although Hallett subsequently tried to get new indictments, he failed and had finally to content himself with Attorney General Cushing's restrained approval of his management of the affair: "The point on which the indictment was held insufficient," Cushing wrote the defeated Hallett, "is of such a nature, that the result cannot justly impair your professional reputation or injure consideration with the Government."[29]

Long Range Dissatisfaction

Even though in the Burns case the federal government had succeeded in enforcing the Fugitive Slave Law, it had failed, here as in the Shadrach, the Christiana, and the Jerry cases, to get the courts to punish those who had defied it. Was it only military force which could make enforcement possible? And if enforcement of civil law depended on the use of martial law, what then? Could a society of laws exist when moral opposition to one law not only made citizens defy it openly but also left courts hesitant to punish its violators? And in that case could the national government afford to ignore the implications? Might not a determined enforcement of the Fugitive Slave Law more effectively destroy the slave interests it was designed to protect than anything their opponents could do?

The sequel to the Burns case threw such questions into sharp relief. As in Syracuse after the rescue of Jerry McHenry, so in Boston after the rendition of Anthony Burns, new private organizations emerged to oppose enforcement of the law. One such new secret society, in appealing for Higginson's membership, seemingly subscribed to more cohesive revolutionary action than the old Vigilance Committee by pledging "to use all proper means for rendering difficult or impossible the coming or the remaining of the Manhunter among us."[30] There was also public action. Boston city aldermen voted to evict the federal courts from the courthouse. At the state level, in 1855 the legislature passed a new and more stringent personal liberty law which, among other provisions, fired any state official issuing a certificate to return a fugitive, barred federal officials authorized to issue such certificates from holding state office, closed practice in state courts to attorneys who acted for the claimants of fugitives, and appointed public defenders in each county to secure fugitives their legal right to jury trial (Document IV-A-2). Though parts of the law were repealed in 1858, only two persons were subsequently returned to slavery from Massachusetts, neither of them by legal process (Document I-A-2).

Of those involved in the Burns affair, excepting Burns himself, the major victim was Commissioner Loring. Within a year, Harvard trustees removed him from his law lectureship, and numerous petitions brought legislative resolutions demanding that he be ousted from his probate judgeship. Though Governor Henry Gardner refused to remove him in 1855, Nathaniel Banks did so in 1858. His subsequent appointment to a federal judgeship offered little solace for his loss of public trust.

Sumner's wish that the "odious Bill" would "be annulled in Mass[achusetts]"[31] was thus largely realized by public and private action. Even more significantly, the Burns affair betokened a pervasive change of mood. Boston's well-known liberal clergyman James Freeman Clarke had attributed the possibility of Burns's rendition to the failure of public opinion and a general lassitude among Bostonians. Yet the fact that it occurred cut deeply into the public conscience. Edward Everett, just come home to Boston after resigning his Senate seat, recognized the change. "However much the anti-slavery agitation . . . is to be deprecated," he wrote in mid-June to his former colleague, Joseph Cottman of Maryland, "it is no longer possible to resist it. A change has taken place in this community within three weeks such as the 30 preceding years had not produced. While the minds of conservative men were embittered by the passage of the Nebraska bill, the occurrence of a successful demand for the Surrender of a fugitive Slave was the last drop, which made the cup run over."[32]

Albert G. Browne, whose son had participated in the charge on the courthouse, came to the same conclusion, though with considerably more pleasure. Sure that the trials of the rescuers would hold the public's sympathetic interest, he concluded that the rendition had served the cause better than a rescue could have for "it has brought many a mind on our side, which nothing else could have done."[33] Others also saw in the court procedures an antislavery weapon. Higginson congratulated Theodore Parker on being indicted, and hoped the case would be both "a triumph for you & us" and an impetus to "a division & perhaps a civil war."[34] Garrison, far more dramatic and public in his response, stood on a platform in Framingham, Massachusetts, on July 4 and waved aloft copies of Commissioner Loring's decision, the judge's charge to one of the grand juries, and the United States Constitution. Then, amid cheers from his abolitionist audience, he burned the documents, one by one.

The intensification of antislavery sentiment and resentment at fugitive law enforcement was clearly perceived in the South. Colonel Suttle's home town paper, the Alexandria, Virginia, *Gazette*, almost echoed Higginson's prediction. "As surely as this game [of open defiance of the law] is commenced," it editorialized, "just so surely will it provoke, and justifiably provoke, retaliation on the part of the South, and the work of *dissolving the Union will commence.*"[35] The Charleston, South Carolina, *Mercury*, the South's most persistent disunionist paper, quoted the Northern press on the unenforcibility of the Fugitive Slave Law and surmised that peace within the Union was a tenuous hope for Southerners. "We look, then," the paper said on June 3, "for a renewal of the struggle. The Boston riot is a link in the chain. It is another warning to the South—another lifting up of the veil of the troubles yet to come."[36] And in Pensacola, Florida, the *Gazette*, less strident than the *Mercury*, could at its most optimistic advise only watchful waiting in a period of great anxiety, hoping that "good may yet come out of this evil."[37]

Beside those for whom disunion was either anticipated or desired stood Southern moderates who, yearning for a peaceful union, equally demanded law and order. A grand jury of the North Carolina federal district court pressed the point when it condemned the attempted Boston rescue and praised Pierce's "promptness and energy in enforcing the laws."[38] And the Charleston *Courier* quoted the Boston *Post* with satisfaction when that paper extolled the "propriety, courage, and wisdom" of Marshal Freeman, who, for his "nerve, intelligence, and fidelity" deserved the "honor and gratitude" of the nation.[39]

But some Southerners, even while they backed federal enforcement of the fugitive law, questioned its effectiveness. Was the government's victory substantive or only illusory? Should the rendition of Anthony Burns reassure them? The Richmond, Virginia, *Enquirer* doubted it. Though it supported the Pierce administration's action, it argued that Southern taxes helped pay the expenses incurred in the Burns case, which were estimated to run as high as $50,000. Could the South afford to pay so heavily for the return of a single slave? And should she pay at all when it was illegal Northern resistance which had made the expense necessary? On a more theoretical level, the *Enquirer* was also uneasy, as were many Northern papers, at the use of force to compel obedience to law. It was, the Virginia editor concluded, contradictory to the concept of free government (Document II-C-3). With equal perception, a South Carolinian studying at Harvard wrote that the rendition gave no reassurance to his section, for it reflected less a spirit of constitutional obligation than a grim determination to maintain order in Boston. "Can any one fail to perceive that the very boast of its enforcement proves the great fear there was, even in their own minds, of its possibility? Can any reflecting Southern man read the facts of this case, and not see, with such associates and rulers, that he verges towards the brink of a horrible and bottomless abyss of infamy and misery?"[40]

Some Final Ironies

Was then the enforcement of the Fugitive Slave Law a hollow mockery? Did the return of Anthony Burns do more to develop antislavery sentiment and nullify the law than the example which Boston had set by open defiance? Did the meaning of the case lie in its substance, or did its significance come only from the conflicting values which it symbolized? That the concern it generated had little to do with Burns is certain. Only three weeks after his slave had marched down State Street, Suttle wrote Hamilton Willis trying to sell him for $1,500. That the original Boston subscribers refused the offer tells equally their disinterest in Burns per se. If Suttle had declined to sell in order to demonstrate that the law could be enforced, Boston merchants had tried to buy to avoid that test. As a result Suttle sold his recaptured runaway to a North Carolina trader for a mere $910. Six months later the trader made a 40 percent profit by selling Burns for $1,300, raised this time largely from Boston's black community. At roughly the same time that Suttle sold Burns, Caleb Cushing, so sure of the law's interpretation in May, sought a Supreme Court decision "whether there be or not any valid constitutional objection to the acts of Congress, making provision for the extradition of fugitives bound to service in any State."[41]

For two weeks Anthony Burns, escaped slave, had been the unwitting center of a drama whose origins, unfolding, and denouement, starkly focussed conflicts and tensions which had strained the national consensus for years. It also tested the will and capacity of government at all levels to enforce law and keep the peace. Yet the formal conclusion of that drama, the rendition of the fugitive, did little to reinforce national unity, reassure the South, or provide for easier law enforcement in the future. In Massachusetts and throughout the North, the case rather catalyzed an increased will to defy the Fugitive Slave Law. And still the questions remain: were there any viable alternatives?

Notes

1. Boston *Evening Journal*, May 27, 1854, reprinted in New York *Daily Times*, May 29, 1854.

2. Charles Emery Stevens, *Anthony Burns. A History* (1856; New York: Negro Universities Press, 1969), 64.

3. New York *Daily Tribune*, May 31, 1854.

4. Washington *Union*, n.d., reprinted in Tallahassee, Florida, *Sentinal*, June 6, 1854.

5. Quoted in Roy Nichols, *Franklin Pierce: Young Hickory of the Granite Hills*, rev. ed. (Philadelphia: University of Pennsylvania Press, 1958), 361.

6. Boston *Evening Transcript*, May 29, 1854.

7. *Ibid.*

8. Robert Manson Myers, ed., *The Children of Pride. A True Story of Georgia and the Civil War* (New Haven: Yale University Press, 1972), 37.

9. Edward G. Parker to Charles J. Lanman, [May 30, 1854]; Norcross Papers, Massachusetts Historical Society.

10. New York *Daily Tribune*, May 31, 1854.

11. *Liberator*, June 2, 1854.

12. New York *Daily Times*, May 30, 1854.

13. Amos A. Lawrence to Giles Richards, June 1, 1854, Letterpress; A.A. Lawrence Papers, Massachusetts Historical Society.

14. Amos A. Lawrence to Brother, May 29, 1854, Letterpress; Lawrence Papers.

15. Amos A. Lawrence to J.V.C. Smith, May 27, 1854, pencilled summary, Letterpress; Lawrence Papers.

16. *The Boston Slave Riot, and Trial of Anthony Burns. . .* (Boston: Fetridge and Company, 1854), 13.

17. George F. Williams to Charles Sumner, June 8, 1854; Sumner Papers, Houghton Library, Harvard University.

18. Franklin Pierce to Benjamin F. Hallett, May 31, 1854, quoted in Stevens, *Burns*, 274.

19. New York *Daily Times*, May 30, 1854.

20. U.S., Congress, Senate, *Congressional Globe*, 31st Cong., 2nd sess., February 21, 1851, Appendix, 300.

21. Watson Freeman to J.V.C. Smith, May 30, 1854, in William H. Ela, *William H. Ela vs. J.V.C. Smith and als. Heard in Norfolk County Supreme Judicial Court, February Term, 1855* [Boston: n.p., 1855].

22. Benjamin F. Hallett to Sidney Webster, May 31, 1854, quoted in Stevens, *Burns,* 274.

23. Stevens, *Burns,* 141.

24. James Freeman Clarke, *The Rendition of Anthony Burns. Its Causes and Consequences...* (Boston: Crosby, Nichols & Co., and Prentiss & Sawyer, 1854), 17.

25. Charleston *Courier,* June 23, 1854.

26. Pensacola *Gazette,* June 3, 1854.

27. New York *Journal of Commerce,* n.d., reprinted in *Liberator,* June 9, 1854.

28. Theodore Parker, *The Trial of Theodore Parker...* (Boston: The Author, 1855), xviii.

29. Caleb Cushing to Benjamin F. Hallett, April 19, 1855, draft. U.S., Department of Justice, Letters Sent by the Attorney-General, Microfilm, T-969, Roll 1. Federal Record Center, Waltham, Massachusetts.

30. Henry J. Bowditch to Thomas W. Higginson, August 10, 1854; in Thomas W. Higginson, comp., Ms Correspondence, etc., Relating to the Anthony Burns Episode, etc., 1851-1900. Antislavery Collection, Boston Public Library.

31. Charles Sumner to Thomas W. Higginson, June 12, 1854, in *ibid.*

32. [Edward Everett] to Joseph S. Cottman, June 15, 1854, Copy; Everett Papers, Microfilm, Reel 30, Massachusetts Historical Society.

33. Albert G. Browne to Thomas W. Higginson, June 16, 1854, in Higginson, Correspondence Relating to Anthony Burns.

34. Thomas W. Higginson to Theodore Parker, December 1, 1854, in *ibid.*

35. Alexandria, Virginia, *Gazette,* n.d., reprinted in Charleston, S.C., *Courier,* June 7, 1854.

36. Charleston *Mercury,* June 3, 1854.

37. Pensacola *Gazette,* June 10, 1854.

38. Charleston *Courier,* June 16, 1854.

39. Boston *Post,* n.d., reprinted in *ibid.,* June 5, 1854.

40. Charleston *Mercury,* June 12, 1854.

41. Caleb Cushing to F.B. Streeter, September 11, 1854; in C.C. Andrews, ed., *Official Opinions of the Attorneys General of the United States* (Washington: Robert Farnham, 1856), 6:714.

part two

Documents of the Decision

In a federal republic, where power is divided among different branches and levels of government, decision making on controversial issues is never simple—or final. And when an issue is laden with questions of moral conviction, economic viability, and the survival of constitutional union, as was that of returning fugitive slaves during the 1850s, assessing governmental and popular response to it becomes extremely complex.

To facilitate such an assessment, the documents which follow have been subdivided in two ways. The first grouping (I, II, III, and IV) defines the various governmental and public levels at which decisions are made and actions taken. The second grouping (A, B, C, D, and E) describes the alternative kinds of actions deemed possible and useful at each level by contemporaries as ways of coping with the problem of the Fugitive Slave Law. How choices among alternatives were ultimately made over time constitutes a third analytic dimension. That is the substance of the preceding narrative text.

Organizational arrangements such as the one used here are the analyst's way of ordering material so as to make it more understandable. In fact it is never quite so tidy, for there is constant interaction among branches of government and the public at large. Such interaction shaped the emotion-laden crisis which, in the Burns case in 1854, seemingly defied satisfactory resolution.

I

Congressional Alternatives

The problem facing the Congress was how to legislate both to insure the carrying out of the constitutional provision for the return of fugitives from labor and to protect the economic security of the South, and, at the same time, how to adjust such legislation to the evident and growing disinclination among Northerners to tolerate the reenslavement of those who had escaped bondage. In seeking a resolution, Congress considered several options, none of which was universally satisfactory.

Alternative A

To make a strict and enforceable fugitive slave law

1. James M. Mason of Virginia served continuously in the House of Representatives or the Senate from 1837 until his expulsion in 1861. Thereafter he became Confederate commissioner to Great Britain and France. As a senator from a border state, Mason was eager to curtail his constituents'

property loss from escaped slaves. He largely drafted the 1850 bill, and, with the help of Senator Andrew P. Butler, chairman of the judiciary committee, shepherded it through the Senate. Here in a Senate debate in 1850, he stressed the need for a new law. (See pages 6-7.)

Document†

If it be intended, as I have no doubt it is, by a majority of the Senate, to pass a law which shall be effectual to execute, in good faith, the Constitution of the United States in reference to fugitives from labor, it is necessary that the Senate should take into view and consider the actual evils under which the slave States labor, in reference to the reclamation of these fugitives. The State from whence I came, and the States of Kentucky and Maryland, being those States of the Union that border on the free States, have had ample experience, not only of the difficulties, but of the actual impossibility of reclaiming a fugitive when he once gets within the boundaries of a non-slaveholding State; and this bill, or rather the amendments which I have offered, have been framed with a great deal of consideration, to reach, if practicable, the evils which this experience has demonstrated to exist, and to furnish the appropriate remedy in enabling the owner of a fugitive to reclaim him. Sir, it has become a part of the history of the country, that, when a slave once escapes and gets within the limits of the free States, or the most of those into which they do escape, for I do not mean or desire to be invidious by particularizing instances, you may as well go down into the sea, and endeavor to recover from his native element a fish which had escaped from you, as expect to recover such fugitive—I mean under existing laws. Every difficulty is thrown in the way by the population to avoid discovery of where he is, and after this discovery is made, every difficulty is thrown in the way of executing process upon him. And if you should succeed so far as to execute the process, then every difficulty is thrown in the way by armed mobs to prevent the fugitive being carried before the proper officer to take cognizance of the case. And, if you should perchance succeed in doing this, and an adjudication should be made, I do not know of an instance, within recent years, where the fugitive was not rescued by violence from the hands of the officer by an armed mob, and the parties claiming him put in peril of their lives. Indeed, in one instance, in Pennsylvania, one of the parties was killed outright by the mob, but in every instance their lives are put in peril. And when, as is sometimes the case, the parties thus aggrieved seek a remedy through civil suits brought against the individuals composing such a mob, after years of vexatious difficulties thrown in the way, they are finally left to pay the costs of the suit. This is the real State of things, and I could give instances which have come under my own knowledge, of owners of slaves who have gone into free States and recaptured their fugitives, which were afterwards rescued from them by violence and force.

†From: U.S. Congress, Senate, *Congressional Globe*, 31st Cong., 2d sess., August 19, 1850, Appendix, p. 1583.

The amendments to the bill which I have offered have been framed in such a manner as, having due and entire regard to the rights of the citizens of those States, to reach all these difficulties, and if possible to remove them, so as to enable the owner to recover his fugitive.

2. Despite congressional efforts in 1850 to make the new Fugitive Slave Law enforceable, the experience of the succeeding four years led the Senate in February 1855 to reconsider the same old issues. Senator James A. Bayard of Delaware supported a bill designed to facilitate administration of the Fugitive Slave Law in states having personal liberty laws by transferring cases connected in any way with its enforcement to federal courts. (See page 50.)

Document†

What is this bill? It arises from a system of legislation which has grown up under the influence of a spirit of fanaticism, a spirit which is striking at the foundations of this Union. Within the last eight or ten years what has been the progress of things? The act of Congress called the fugitive slave law was modified, was made practically enforcible, no more. None of its essential principles were altered from the time of its first enactment to the passage of the amended law of 1850. When that law was passed, the first steps of the honorable Senator's* coadjutors, and those who think with them, were open resistance to the law. They went even so far as to murder an officer of the United States in the performance of his duty.** But, sir, prudence taught them that this species of resistance to the laws of the United States, under any plea of philanthropy, or whatever they cloaked it under, would never be sanctioned by the sentiment of the people of the country. Finding that to be so, they have since resorted to another mode of nullifying and rendering nugatory the constitutional laws of the United States, and that is by State enactment. . . . Some States, I have said, have passed laws with a view to render that law nugatory . . . which, on the face of their provisions, are shocking to all principles of justice; laws which, among other provisions, contain this one: that if a man makes a claim to property recognized by the Constitution and laws of his country as property, capable of existence, and if, by any accident, (for no exception is made of the death of his witness, or the perjury of the opposing party's witness, or of any other cause whatever,) he fails to support his claim, he is to be imprisoned in the State prison as a convicted felon because of the unsuccessful attempt to assert his rights!

When such laws as that are passed, with all the influence of some State Legislatures, to prevent, and intended to prevent, carrying into execution the laws of the United States, made under the Constitution, is it not a sufficient reason why the Congress of the United States, having the constitutional power, should interpose, not for the purpose of aggression on the rights of any State, but simply in

†From: U.S., Congress, Senate, *Congressional Globe*, 33d Cong., 2d sess., February 23, 1855, Appendix, pp. 243-44.

*Here Bayard is responding to Senator William H. Seward of New York.

**John Batchelder, killed during the attempt to rescue Anthony Burns.

order to say that the officer, who is to carry out their law, and those who aid that officer, if sued in a civil action for anything done under any law of the United States, shall have the election of giving security and transferring jurisdiction to the Federal court, or allowing the suit to proceed to trial in the State court? That is all we propose. . . . We have shown a state of facts justifying this. There is a party who first attempted an organized opposition to this Government. I will not speak of their motives; but certainly, if their objects be effected, this Union must certainly be at an end. An organized party has grown up, formidable I admit—and I admit it with sorrow and regret—which first attempted to put at defiance a law by mobs and by murder. They found that there was yet remaining too much attachment to the Union, and they had so much reflective power remaining themselves as to see that four or five instances of that kind would necessarily make their fellows stop and inquire into the motives of the action of men who used such a mode of proceeding to sustain their opinions. Then they have had resort to State legislative action for the purpose of attaining the same object which they first sought to attain by open resistance to the laws.

It is to meet that contingency that the present bill has become imperative, and is within the terms of the Constitution, fully and to its broadest extent.

Alternative B

To assure alleged fugitive slaves the judicial process guaranteed to others

1. William H. Seward of New York, a freshman senator in 1850, came to Washington prepared to introduce legislation protecting the rights of alleged fugitives. He already had a reputation as a leading antislavery politician, gained when as governor of his state, he had refused to extradite to Virginia and Georgia New York sailors accused of stealing slaves by aiding them to escape. The following are the major operative sections of the amendment to the fugitive slave bill which he offered in the Senate on January 28, 1850. (See page 8.)

Document†

When any person who shall have been seized or arrested as a fugitive from labor, under or by virtue of the act of Congress entitled "An act respecting fugitives from justice and persons escaping from the service of their masters," passed February 12th, 1793, shall be brought or come before any judge or magistrate named or described in said act, the person so arrested or seized may deny that he owes such service or labor as is alledged, or that he has escaped from such service or labor: it shall be the duty of such judge or magistrate thereupon to appoint a time and place to try the issue thus joined; and adjournments shall be granted from time to time, as shall be found to be

†From: U.S., Congress, Senate, *Congressional Globe*. 31st Cong., 1st sess., January 28, 1850, p. 236.

necessary for the furtherance of a just decision upon the fact; and the person so arrested may give bail or security, to be approved by said judge or magistrate, for his appearance at such adjournment, if it shall be granted on his application; and the claimants shall give security to the person so arrested or seized, for the payment of damages and costs, if the claim shall be adjudged void; such security shall be approved in like manner as aforesaid.

And the issue thus joined shall be tried before a jury of twelve persons duly qualified to serve as jurors for the district, free from all challenges or just exceptions, to be summoned by the marshal of the district by virtue of a venire,* to be issued by such judge or magistrate; and exceptions may be taken by either party on such trial, and judgment shall be rendered for or against the claimant according as the verdict shall be.

. . .

Be it enacted by the authority aforesaid, That any person arrested or seized as a fugitive from labor or service, shall be entitled to a writ of habeas corpus, to be issued by the judge of the district court or any associate justice of the Supreme Court of the United States, as a writ of right; and on being brought before such judge by virtue of said writ, it shall be the duty of such judge to proceed to a trial of the claim by jury in the manner before mentioned, if no trial has been had, and to discharge him from such arrest, if such trial by jury has been had, and the claim has not been sustained before the jury or the court which had cognizance of the same.

2. The Pennsylvania Society for Promoting the Abolition of Slavery, the Relief of Free Negroes unlawfully held in Bondage, and Improving the Condition of the African Race, founded in 1775, was one of the oldest antislavery organizations in the country. On January 31, 1853, Senator John P. Hale, recently defeated presidential candidate of the Free Soil party, presented the society's petition to amend the 1850 Fugitive Slave Law so as to guarantee defendants under it specific legal rights. This was but one of many such petitions seeking either amendment or repeal of the law. (See page 14.)

Document†
In pursuance of their purpose they respectfully call the attention of the Senate and the House of Representatives to the act of Congress passed in September, 1850, known as the fugitive slave law, which, not only by its entire omission to throw any guards around the rights of the unfortunate class upon whom it is designed to operate, but also by its open violation of those fundamental principles which were deemed by all the framers of the Constitution necessary to protect the rights of the free-born citizen, is especially calculated to inflict flagrant wrong upon that oppressed and persecuted class of inhabitants. By article three, section one, of the

---

*A writ calling a number of qualified persons to serve as jurors.

†From: U.S., Congress, Senate, *Congressional Globe.* 32d Cong., 2d sess., January 31, 1853, pp. 450-51.

Constitution, it is provided that "the judicial power of the United States shall be vested in one Supreme Court, and in such inferior courts as Congress may from time to time ordain and establish. The judges, both of the supreme and inferior courts, shall hold their offices during good behavior, and shall, at stated times, receive for their services a compensation which shall not be diminished during their continuance in office." And by article five of the amendments thereto, it is provided that no person shall be "deprived of life, liberty, or property, without due process of law." And yet by the fugitive slave law the exercise of the highest judicial authority is conferred upon an irresponsible individual unknown to the Constitution. The power of deciding upon *ex parte* testimony, and without appeal, the right of any person who may be thrown before him to that "blessing of liberty," to secure which the Constitution was ordained and established, is vested in a subordinate officer of an inferior court, with a contingent fee for his services in deciding against the inalienable right of all men. The memorialists therefore earnestly request Congress to take measures for the immediate repeal of that law, or such modification of it as may be necessary to protect the rights of freemen by conforming its operation to the principles of the common law and the theory of the Government.

Alternative C

To realize that no law could be enforced against public opinion

1. In an exchange on the floor of the Senate during the debates which preceded the passage of the fugitive slave bill, two moderate Whigs, Thomas G. Pratt of Maryland and Robert C. Winthrop of Massachusetts, discussed how to deal with popular opposition to a law which both men wanted to make enforceable. Winthrop, a Cotton Whig recently appointed to the Senate to replace Daniel Webster, was in the particularly difficult position of representing a state which was both a hotbed of abolitionism and a bulwark of cotton trade and manufacture. Pratt's solution to the dilemma is in I-D-1. (See page 8.)

Document†

Mr. WINTHROP. Then I am to understand the Senator from Maryland [Pratt] to advance the very reverse of my proposition, and to imply that, whenever we desire to have any law on this or any other subject faithfully executed, we should frame its provisions in utter disregard of the views, feelings, and sense of justice of the people over whom that law is to operate. That would seem to be the implication from his argument; for, while I maintain that with a view of carrying out a law effectually we must in some degree consult the views and principles of the community in which it is to be

†From: U.S., Congress, Senate, *Congressional Globe* 31st Cong., 1st sess., August 20, 1850, Appendix, p. 1592.

enforced, the Senator says, as I understand him, that he would be quite ashamed of the people of Maryland if they were to hold to any such doctrine. Why, sir, for what are we sent here? I supposed it was to represent the people—to represent the views and principles of the people in the various parts of the country from which we come. I supposed that we were sent here to embody those views and principles, so far as we can do so, consistently with our allegiance to the Constitution of the United States, in the laws which we may pass and promulgate. . . .

Mr. PRATT. Now, how could the Senator understand me to say that the true policy for Congress to pursue, in order to have the laws executed, was to pass them in opposition to the sentiments of the people where they were to be executed? . . . I said that the people of Maryland, to use his own language, would be ashamed, would consider themselves traitors to the country, if they attempted, influenced by their own feelings, before the law had been adjudicated to be unconstitutional, to invalidate a law passed by Congress. He says—and we all know that his people and the people of the North generally, on this particular subject, have set at defiance and at naught the constitutional law passed by Congress on the subject of fugitive slaves—the execution of the law depends on the feelings of the people where it is to be executed; and that, the will of his people being against the execution of this law, it cannot be executed there. I said, on the contrary, that, however a law might be against the feelings of the people of my State, they will yet allow it to be executed, until it is decided by the Supreme Court, the proper tribunal, to be unconstitutional. That is the difference between us.

. . .

Mr. WINTHROP. Sir, I hold with the Senator from Maryland himself that no people are at liberty to set aside a law as unconstitutional until it has been decided to be unconstitutional by the Supreme Court of the United States. No man goes further in that doctrine than I do, and the Senator, it seems to me, has really misunderstood the whole idea and character of my remarks. I was arguing no matter of principle. I was arguing a question of fact, a question of practical experience; and my position was, that, if you wish a law to be faithfully executed, you must conform it in some degree to the views of the people upon whom it is to operate. Can anybody deny this? Why, sir, it is the daily experience of this and of every other Government, that, when laws are repugnant to the moral sense of the people it is almost impossible to execute them. I said nothing to justify disobedience. I merely maintained that, if the provisions of a statute for the recapture of fugitives were conformed to the sense of justice of the community in which those fugitives had taken refuge, they would be more likely to be recovered by their owners, than under laws which violate all those great principles of free government upon which we ourselves rely for our own individual security.

2. South Carolina's Andrew P. Butler, who, as chairman of the Senate Judiciary Committee, was officially responsible for presenting the 1850 fugitive slave bill and guiding it through to passage, doubted at the time that

any such law could be effective. Shortly after the dramatic rescue of Shadrach in Boston, on February 18, 1851, he reassessed the relative responsibility for enforcement or violation of the law of federal officials and those who shaped Northern public opinion. (See page 17.)

Document†

I will make another remark in connection with this subject. I do it with a firm belief of its truth. That in Boston, in the community of Massachusetts, you may throw as much blame on the marshal as you think proper, but the Federal officers will find it impossible by their mere exertion of power to carry into effect this article of the Constitution, and the law referred to for the purpose of giving force to it. If they cannot call out the *posse comitatus*, the very highest power which a sheriff or a marshal has, it is in vain for them to resort to Federal agencies as a limited and impotent means to perform the duties of their offices. Why, you are now attempting by auxiliary legislation to do, what? To breathe life into an extinct article of the Constitution of the United States. You are to supply from time to time, from session to session, acts of legislation to compel people who are opposed to the Constitution to observe it—to resort to the Army and Navy, to military force, to compel citizens to the duty which honor, honesty, justice, and good faith had previously imposed upon them. It is perfectly in vain, as has been said, in consequence of the sentiment which obtains in some of the northern States, and especially in Massachusetts, with the limited number of officers and the limited power which they exert over the community, to enforce this article of the Constitution. Sir, they are reconciled by a mere casuistry to see it violated; they are reconciled to it by the pulpit; they are reconciled to it by designing politicians; and so long as the question of slavery forms an element of political agitation, you might as well attempt to hush the winds by saying to them "cease." As I said the other day, you might as well expect to keep a maniac quiet by singing lullabies as to undertake in this way to compel a reluctant people to do their duty.

Alternative D

To find some sort of compromise

1. Senator Thomas G. Pratt of Maryland contended, in his speech on August 20, 1850, defending his proposed amendment to the fugitive slave bill, that both the problem and its solution were economic in nature. Thus he sought to avoid the difficulties presented by principle and moral conviction as they related to law enforcement, which he and Massachusetts Senator Winthrop debated in I-C-1. (See page 9.)

---

†From: U.S., Congress, Senate, *Congressional Globe*. 31st Cong., 2d sess., February 21, 1851, Appendix, p. 298.

Document†

Now, sir, the amendment which I have had the honor to propose is predicated upon this proposition, that, where, as here, there is a clear, distinct, manifest obligation imposed by the Constitution in reference to property therein recognized as such, to deliver up that property to the owner, when claimed by him, there follows, as a consequence of a neglect to perform that duty, an obligation on the parties upon whom it is imposed to pay for the property. I apprehend that no proposition can be clearer than this, that where any competent authority imposes on an individual a binding, legal, constitutional obligation to do a particular thing, to deliver up to an individual property which belongs to him, that, from the nondischarge upon the part of the individual of the obligation so imposed, there would necessarily result a liability on the part of the individual to pay the damage or loss consequent to the owner. I think that there is no legal mind in the Senate, no member of the Senate, who will deny this proposition. I apprehend also, that the further proposition cannot be denied, that where an obligation imposed on an individual is binding, the same obligation would be binding if imposed in the same language upon the Federal Government. Here, then, I have made out, I think, that under the Constitution, and the construction of that Constitution by the Supreme Court of the United States, the Government of the United States had assumed the obligation to deliver to the owners of fugitive slaves those slaves, whenever claimed by the owners. Now, I say that no mind, as it appears to me, can dissent from the conclusion that the noncompliance by the Federal Government with the obligation so imposed, would necessarily devolve upon the Government the obligation to pay the master for the loss which he may have sustained by reason of this dereliction of duty on the part of that Government. The principle of the amendment is based upon this theory.

If I might claim the indulgence of the Senate, I would be glad, for a very few moments, to call their attention to the subject—or one of the subjects—which has been under discussion for the last six months, for the purpose of showing that the amendment which I have proposed is one which would tend more effectually to establish peace and harmony between the two sections of the country than any of those hitherto acted on by this body. It was well said by the Senator from Massachusetts [Mr. WINTHROP] yesterday, that there are people, both North and South, who desire the separation of this Union, and the destruction of the Federal Government. Those at the North have been actuated by a wish to abolish slavery, and their desire to destroy the Government proceeds from the proclaimed fact, on their part, that the Constitution of the United States protects the master in his right to his slave as property, and the consequent inability, on their part, to abolish slavery. This, then, is the fanatic notion of those persons at the North, who desire to destroy the Government of the country. Now, there is a class of

†From: U.S., Congress, Senate, *Congressional Globe.* 31st Cong., 1st sess., August 20, 1850, Appendix, pp. 1591-92.

persons at the South, who, for reasons the exact opposite of those which have induced northern men to entertain these opinions, look to the Government of the country with like aversion, and think that a dissolution of this Union would be of advantage to the South, because this description of property would be better protected under a separate southern government, than it is protected now under the Federal Government. And why, sir? Mr. President, these dangers to the institutions of our country have grown out of the daily excitement which is attempted to be produced, here and elsewhere, upon this subject. We find petitions flowing in here daily, from the northern section of our Union, asking that this property belonging to the South shall be rendered useless to them. It must be recollected by Senators, that the value of this property at the South is estimated at $1,600,000,000. Now, when that is brought to the consideration of the Senate—when members reflect that there is a portion of this country owning a description of property valued at $1,600,000,000, and that daily efforts are made here to induce a state of public opinion by which that large amount of property is to be rendered valueless, they cannot help seeing that there is just cause for excitement on the part of the South. Every one knows that the constitutional provision, and the act of 1793, which I have called to the notice of the Senate, have not afforded an adequate remedy to the South, in reference to their slaves who have escaped from them. Now, the question submitted to the Senate by the amendment I have proposed, is, whether they are willing to protect the South in this admitted constitutional right; and, if they do not pass a law sufficiently efficient to carry out the obligation on the part of the Federal Government to deliver to the owner his slaves, when they escape, whether they will not pay the owner out of the coffers of the National Treasury for the noncompliance with that obligation?

. . .

The American people are essentially a practical people. I never shall believe that they are willing to risk the destruction of this Government upon a mere abstraction.

2. Senator Andrew P. Butler of South Carolina feared both the economic results of Pratt's proposed amendment to the fugitive slave bill (I-D-1) and its broader social implications. Opposition from supporters and opponents of the fugitive slave bill combined to defeat Pratt's proposal to compensate slave owners under certain conditions, for they largely agreed with Butler's analysis of the amendment's implications for the federal treasury. (See page 9.)

Document†

If once you allow, by this prospect of indemnity by the Government, the owner of a slave to be relieved from the absolute necessity of either obtaining his property or of suffering the loss, you destroy essentially all

†From: U.S., Congress, Senate, *Congressional Globe.* 31st Cong., 1st sess., August 19, 1850, Appendix, p. 1598.

incentive to pursuit. When a slave is gone, and the master finds he cannot obtain possession of him—and that with the master will often be a mere matter of opinion—what is he to do? Why, sir, some men who might not be very conscientious, or who might be *very conscientious*, looking to the higher law—for some men's nature differs even in this respect—some men might go, after very little effort to recover the slave, and swear that they had made all proper exertions for his recovery, and with a provision of this kind they would rest perfectly contented with the smallest modicum of exertion which would satisfy their consciences. I am speaking now of those who are supposed to be honest. But, sir, there are, too, dishonest masters, who might make collusions with their slaves to runaway, so that they might thus obtain an overrated value for them; and others, again, who, while they would not have any collusion with their slaves, might still be willing that they should escape, knowing that they would be paid for them by the Federal Government. And that, sir, it seems to me, is the most obvious mode of inducing slaves to escape, and is one of the modes of emancipation which some enthusiasts would hail with thanksgiving, and the only guard against it would be that so many slaves would escape to the non-slaveholding States that the people there would be obliged to expel them. It would increase the evil, too, in the border States, which would soon be emptied of the slaves now there, only to make way for others. This might not be the immediate effect of such a provision, but there can be no question that such would be its ultimate operation; and the Federal Treasury would have to pay every year more and more, for what? Why, because the master who loses a slave is to be paid the value of him by the Federal Government, provided he cannot obtain him; and the Government is to make good the loss which arises from the fault of the State which chooses, by its authorities, to give him refuge and protection. I have heard of a principle of law that every hundred should be good for any robbery committed in it, and a good law it might be. And if you can make the States into which the fugitive has fled liable for his loss, there might be reason in it. With such a law you would make the States interested in rendering up these fugitives. But, by adopting the provision suggested, you would destroy that principle altogether, and throw the whole upon this good "milch cow," the Federal Government.

Alternative E

To leave the return of fugitives to the constitutional provision and state action

1. Senator James Mason of Virginia argued during the final weeks of debate on the fugitive slave bill that should Northern citizens and state governments fail to enforce the bill that he had fathered, redress would necessarily lie with action by the Southern states. (See page 11.)

Document†

Now, Mr. President, as I have said, I am perfectly aware of the feelings of the people of my own State upon the subject of these losses. They have become too onerous and too heavy to be borne, and are increasing from year to year. They have been estimated upon such data as have been afforded through the newspapers and other sources of information on the subject, and they are put down by gentlemen of intelligence as exceeding a hundred thousand dollars annually, which losses are sustained by our citizens, because the law fails to protect their property. These losses fall upon citizens who have been taught obedience to the law, taught to look to the law as the protector of their property; and when they ask for redress they are referred, not to their own State, because the Constitution of the United States has taken from their own State all power to protect them; they are pointed to the Constitution of the United States; and if Congress declares by their refusal to make this provision, or some equivalent one, that they have discharged all their duty when they have enacted a law, whether it be executed or not, I say again, it will devolve upon the States to protect their citizens as best they may. It will devolve upon the Legislatures of the several States to devise the means of protection, and not to rely upon Congress. If we are driven to that ultimately, I need not say what alienation of feeling, what hostile acts may result between State and State, and between the citizens of one State and those of another, in attempts to obtain that redress which has been refused by Congress. Whether this protection can be given by the States I do not know, but I have the strongest reason to know that it will be attempted. It is asking too much of the intelligent citizens of any well-organized State at this time, of any State whose legal morals are sound, to require of them to submit to such losses, by saying to them we are not able to afford you any redress.

2. Antislavery radical Charles Sumner of Massachusetts pressed home the strict states' rights objection to the Fugitive Slave Law which antislavery Whigs and Democrats both used in opposing a variety of federal legislation touching slavery. In his August 26, 1852 Senate speech he proposed the repeal of the law and rang the changes on the popular Free Democratic slogan—"Freedom, national; slavery, sectional." (See pages 22, 27-28.)

Document††

We have seen that any compromise, finally closing the discussion of slavery under the Constitution, is tyrannical, absurd, and impotent; that as slavery can exist only by virtue of positive law, and as it has no such positive

†From: U.S., Congress, Senate, *Congressional Globe.* 31st Cong., 1st sess., August 21, 1850, Appendix, p. 1605.

††From: U.S., Congress, Senate, *Congressional Globe.* 32d Cong., 1st sess., August 26, 1852, Appendix, pp. 1112, 1113.

support in the Constitution, it cannot exist within the national jurisdiction; that the Constitution nowhere recognizes property in man, and that, according to its true interpretation, freedom and not slavery is national, while slavery and not freedom is sectional; that, in this spirit, the National Government was first organized under Washington, himself an abolitionist, surrounded by abolitionists, while the whole country, by its church, its colleges, its literature, and all its best voices, was united against slavery, and the national flag at that time nowhere within the national territory covered a single slave; still further, that the National Government is a Government of delegated powers, and as among these there is no power to support slavery, this institution cannot be national, nor can Congress in any way legislate in its behalf; and, finally, that the establishment of this principle is the true way of peace and safety for the Republic. Considering next the provision for the surrender of fugitives from labor, we have seen that it was not one of the original compromises of the Constitution; that it was introduced tardily and with hesitation, and adopted with little discussion, and then and for a long period after was regarded with comparative indifference; that the recent slave act, though many times unconstitutional, is especially so on two grounds—*first*, as a usurpation by Congress of powers not granted by the Constitution, and an infraction of rights secured to the States; and, *secondly*, as a denial of trial by jury, in a question of personal liberty and a suit at common law; that its glaring unconstitutionality finds a prototype in the British stamp act, which our fathers refused to obey as unconstitutional on two parallel grounds—*first*, because it was a usurpation by Parliament of powers not belonging to it under the British Constitution, and an infraction of rights belonging to the Colonies; and *secondly*, because it was a denial of trial by jury in certain cases of property; that as liberty is far above property, so is the outrage perpetrated by the American Congress far above that perpetrated by the British Parliament; and, finally, that the slave act has not that support in the public sentiment of the States where it is to be executed, which is the life of all law, and which prudence and the precept of Washington require.

Sir, thus far I have arrayed the objections to this act, and the false interpretations out of which it has sprung. But I am asked what I offer as a substitute for the legislation which I denounce. Freely I will answer. It is to be found in a correct appreciation of the provision of the Constitution, under which this discussion occurs. Look at it in the double light of reason and of freedom, and we cannot mistake the exact extent of its requirements. Here is the provision:

No person held to service or labor in one State, under the laws thereof, escaping into another, shall, in consequence of any law or regulation therein, be discharged from such service or labor, but shall be delivered up on claim of the party to whom such service or labor may be due.

From the very language employed it is obvious that this is merely a *compact* between the States, with a *prohibition* on the States, *conferring no power on the nation*. In its natural signification it is a compact. According to the example of other countries, and the principles of jurisprudence, it is a compact. . . .

As a compact, its execution depends absolutely upon the States, without any intervention of the nation. *Each State, in the exercise of its own judgment, will determine for itself the precise extent of the obligations assumed.* As a compact in derogation of freedom, it must be construed strictly in every respect—leaning always in favor of freedom, and shunning any meaning not clearly obvious, which takes away important personal rights; mindful that the parties to whom it is applicable are regarded as "persons," of course with all the rights of "persons" under the Constitution; and especially mindful of the vigorous maxim of the common law, that he is cruel and impious who does not always favor freedom. With this key, the true interpretation is natural and easy.

II

Administrative Alternatives

Enacting sound legislation was only part of the fugitive slave issue. Equally important was administering the law; and that task fell largely to the president, his cabinet officers, and other appointed officials. Their decisions, however, were complicated by pressures from Congress, by the necessities of party politics, and by the course of events—especially recurring defiance of the law.

Alternative A

To execute the Fugitive Slave Law in a firm but customary executive manner

1. In his first annual address to the Congress, less than three months after he had signed the Fugitive Slave Law, President Millard Fillmore made clear the spirit in which he intended to enforce the law. (See page 16.)

Document†

The Constitution has made it the duty of the President to take care that the laws be faithfully executed. In a government like ours, in which all laws are passed by a majority of the representatives of the people, and these representatives are chosen for such short periods that any injurious or obnoxious law can very soon be repealed, it would appear unlikely that any great numbers should be found ready to resist the execution of the laws. But it must be borne in mind that the country is extensive; that there may be local interests or prejudices rendering a law odious in one part which is not so in another, and that the thoughtless and inconsiderate, misled by their passions or their imaginations, may be induced madly to resist such laws as they disapprove. Such persons should recollect that without law there can be no real practical liberty; that when law is trampled under foot tyranny rules, whether it appears in the form of a military despotism or of popular violence. The law is the only sure protection of the weak and the only efficient restraint upon the strong. When impartially and faithfully administered, none is beneath its protection and none above its control. You, gentlemen, and the country may be assured that to the utmost of my ability and to the extent of the power vested in me I shall at all times and in all places take care that the laws be faithfully executed. In the discharge of this duty, solemnly imposed upon me by the Constitution and by my oath of office, I shall shrink from no

†From: James D. Richardson, comp., *A Compilation of the Messages and Papers of the Presidents. . .,* 20 vols. (New York: Bureau of National Literature, 1897-1917), 6:2616.

responsibility, and shall endeavor to meet events as they may arise with firmness, as well as with prudence and discretion.

2. Even as a candidate for the Democratic presidential nomination—though in the excerpt which follows he denied that he was one—Fillmore's successor, Franklin Pierce, felt obliged to reassure the South that his New Hampshire origins would not impede his enforcement of laws which the South deemed crucial. (See page 23.)

Document†

If the compromise measures are not to be substantially and firmly maintained, the plain rights secured by the constitution will be trampled in the dust. What difference can it make to you or me whether the outrage shall seem to fall on South Carolina, or Maine, or New Hampshire? Are not the rights of each equally dear to us all? I will never yield to a craven spirit that, from considerations of policy, would endanger the Union. Entertaining these views, the action of the Convention must, in my judgment, be vital. If we of the North, who have stood by the constitutional rights of the South, are to be abandoned to any time-serving policy, the hopes of Democracy and of the Union must sink together. As I told you, my name will not be before the Convention, but I cannot help feeling that what there is to be done, will be important beyond men and parties—transcendently important to the hopes of Democratic progress, and public liberty.

3. Edward G. Loring, the federal commissioner who presided over the Anthony Burns hearings, justified his ruling on the grounds of the nature of the administrative duties which the Fugitive Slave Law assigned to one holding such office. In his decision he carefully separated the "ministerial" or executive function from the judicial function, which, as a judge, he would serve. (See page 46.)

Document††

The issue between the parties arises under the U.S. Statute of 1850, and for the respondent it is urged that the statute is unconstitutional. Whenever this objection is made it becomes necessary to recur to the purpose of the statute. It purports to carry into execution the provision of the constitution which provides for the extradition of persons held to service or labor in one State and escaping to another. It is applicable, and it is applied alike to bond and free—to the apprentice and the slave, and in reference to both, its purpose, provisions and processes are the same.

The arrest of the fugitive is a ministerial, and not a judicial act, and the nature of the act is not altered by the means employed for its accomplish-

†From: Franklin Pierce to Major Lally, May 27, 1852 in Richmond, Virginia, *Enquirer* June 12, 1852.

††From: "The Decision of Commissioner Loring," in *The Boston Slave Riot and Trial of Anthony Burns...* (Boston: Fetridge and Company, 1854), p. 80.

ment. When an officer arrests a fugitive from justice or a party accused, the officer must determine the identity, and use his discretion and information for the purpose. When an arrest is made under this statute, the means of determining the identity are prescribed by the statute; but when the means are used and the act done, it is still a ministerial act. The statute only substitutes the means it provides for the discretion of an arresting officer, and thus gives to the fugitive from service a much better protection than a fugitive from justice can claim under any law.

If extradition is the only purpose of the statute and the determination of the identity is the only purpose of these proceedings under it, it seems to me that the objection of unconstitutionality to the statute, because it does not furnish a jury trial to the fugitive, is answered; there is no provision in the Constitution requiring the *identity* of the person to be arrested should be determined by a jury. It has never been claimed for apprentices nor fugitives from justice, and if it does not belong to them it does not belong to the respondent.

And if extradition is a ministerial act, to substitute in its performance, for the discretion of an arresting officer, the discretion of a Commissioner instructed by testimony under oath, seems scarcely to reach to a grant of judicial power, within the meaning of the U.S. Constitution. And it is certain that if the power given to and used by the Commissioner of U.S. Courts under the statute is unconstitutional—then so was the power given to, and used by magistrates of counties, cities, and towns, and used by the act of 1793. These all were Commissioners of the United States—the powers they used under the statute were not derived from the laws of their respective States, but from the statute of the United States. They were commissioned by that and that alone. They were commissioned by the class instead of individually and by name, and in this respect the only difference that I can see between the acts of 1793 and 1850 is, that the latter reduced the number of appointees, and confined the appointment to those who by their professional standing should be competent to the performance of their duties, and who bring to them the certificates of the highest judicial tribunals of the land.

Alternative B

To use all governmental force—including the military

1. Millard Fillmore, who in December 1850 had considered enforcement of the Fugitive Slave Law only part of the routine obligation of the president, responded very differently after Boston blacks rescued Fred Wilkins (Shadrach) from a federal courtroom. In his report of the event to the Senate, dated February 19, 1851, he asked the Congress to extend his power so that he could more readily call upon the militia when defiance of the law threatened. At issue was a question both of timing and of prior notice for such action, which a law passed in 1795 just after the Whiskey Rebellion had specified. (See page 17.)

Document†

In regard to the last branch of the inquiry made by the resolution of the Senate, I have to observe that the Constitution declares that "the President shall take care that the laws be faithfully executed," and that "he shall be commander-in-chief of the Army and Navy of the United States, and of the militia of the several States, when called into the actual service of the United States;" and that "Congress shall have power to provide for calling forth the militia to execute the laws of the Union, suppress insurrection, and repel invasions." From which it appears that the Army and Navy are, by the Constitution, placed under the control of the Executive, and probably no legislation of Congress could add to or diminish the power thus given, but by increasing or diminishing or abolishing altogether the Army and Navy. But not so with the militia. The President cannot call the militia into service, even to execute the laws or repel invasions, but by the authority of acts of Congress passed for that purpose. But when the militia are called into service, in the manner prescribed by law, then the Constitution itself gives the command to the President. Acting on this principle, the Congress, by the act of February 28, 1795, authorized the President to call forth the militia to repel invasion and "suppress insurrections against a State government, and to suppress combinations against the laws of the United States, and cause the laws to be faithfully executed." But the act proceeds to declare that, whenever it may be necessary, in the judgment of the President, to use the military force thereby directed to be called forth, the President shall forthwith, by proclamation, command such insurgents to disperse, and retire peaceably to their respective abodes, within a limited time. These words are broad enough to require a proclamation in all cases where militia are called out under that act, whether to repel invasion or suppress an insurrection, or to aid in executing the laws. This section has, consequently, created some doubt whether the militia could be called forth to aid in executing the laws without a previous proclamation. But yet the proclamation seems to be in words directed only against insurgents, and to require them to disperse, thereby implying not only an insurrection, but an organized, or at least an embodied force. Such a proclamation in aid of the civil authority would often defeat the whole object by giving such notice to persons intended to be arrested that they would be enabled to fly or secrete themselves. The force may be wanted sometimes to make the arrest, and also sometimes to protect the officer after it is made, and to prevent a rescue. I would therefore suggest that this section be modified, by declaring that nothing therein contained shall be construed to require any previous proclamation, when the militia are called forth either to repel invasion, to execute the laws, or suppress combinations against them; and that the President may make such call, and place such militia under the control of any civil officer of the United States, to aid him in executing the laws or suppressing such combinations; and while so employed, they shall be paid by and subsisted at the expense of the United States.

†From: U.S., Congress, Senate, *Congressional Globe*. 31st Cong., 2d sess., February 21, 1851, Appendix, p. 293.

2. Congress's failure to pass the legislation President Fillmore sought to facilitate his using the militia to enforce the Fugitive Slave Law (II-C gives the nature of the opposition), cast doubt upon the federal government's power to use either state militia or the army and navy in the Anthony Burns case. On the Saturday following the attempt to storm the Boston courtnouse, however, Attorney General Caleb Cushing issued an opinion which got around the obstacles Fillmore had perceived to calling up troops to enforce federal laws. Interestingly, the opinion was addressed to Secretary of the Interior Robert McClelland in a letter dated May 27, 1854, rather than to President Pierce. Interestingly, too, it was worded so as to appear to be a long delayed response to a communication from McClelland dated four months earlier concerning a fugitive slave case in Chicago. Neither vagary obscured the fact that it was a speedily drawn document designed to justify both the measures which Marshal Watson Freeman had already taken and subsequent steps which Pierce either ordered or approved. At issue was not only the power to enlist troops in a marshal's posse but also the obligation to pay for their services in such a capacity. (See pages 41-42.)

Document†

I repeat, the *posse comitatus* to aid the officer of the law in the execution of his duty is in the service of the Government, not in the service of the individual who sues out the process of the law to have the justice of the nation administered to him, which administration is of the duty of the Government. To guard against violence by wrongheaded, misguided, disloyal citizens, or by foreign force, is an important obligation of every Government,—the grand purpose and consideration, indeed, for which it is instituted. Hence, when the officer of the law deems it necessary and proper to raise the *posse comitatus,* to aid and assist him in executing the process of the law, the extraordinary expense thereby incurred is properly payable by the Government. Expenses to be paid by the parties litigant are ordinary fees, certainly fixed and taxable, as costs against the party at whose particular instance the ordinary services, in the usual calm and peaceful administration of justice, have been performed, and which the successful litigant recovers of his adversary, as taxed costs for his personal wrong and injury. But it would be contrary to all reason, and wholly unjust, to burden either party with the extraordinary expenses incurred by the officer of the law in raising the *posse comitatus,* and keeping them in his employment for five days, or more, in aiding him to perform his duty in obedience to the precept of the law, and in defending its process against the threatened tumults and riotous conduct of lawless men.

The expense, as we have seen, of the sheriff's bailiff [in England], in raising a *posse comitatus* of three hundred men with coats of mail, guns, and

†From: *Official Opinions of the Attorneys General of the United States.* Vol. 6, C.C. Andrews, ed. (Washington: Robert Farnham, 1856), pp. 272-74.

colors, in complete military array . . . were not chargeable to the plaintiff, . . . but the conduct of the sheriff's bailiff, in levying at the public charge such a force, to assist and enable him to do his duty as a public officer, was adjudged lawful. . . .

These considerations apply as well to the military as to the civil force employed; for the *posse comitatus* comprises every person in the district or county above the age of fifteen years . . . whatever may be their occupation, whether civilians or not; and including the military of all denominations, militia, soldiers, marines, all of whom are alike bound to obey the commands of a sheriff or marshal. The fact that they are organized as military bodies, under the immediate command of their own officers, does not in any wise affect their legal character. They are still the *posse comitatus*.

Viewing the several sections of the act of September 18th, 1850, together, as one whole . . . my opinion, therefore, is, that, "assuming that the expenses" in the case of the arrest of the fugitive at Chicago, "were incurred by the marshal in raising the *posse* of his district to aid him in the execution of the warrant against a threatened rescue, prior to the issuing, by the commissioner, of the certificate surrendering the slave to the claimants," still such expenses are "chargeable to the United States, the same as if incurred after the issuing of the certificate."

. . .

This statute of 1850 is enacted to execute a provision of the Constitution, the due and complete execution of which intimately concerns the fate of the Government of the United States and the integrity of the Union. Such a statute deserves, and will receive, a beneficial construction, so that the mischiefs intended to be guarded against may be suppressed by the full use of all the remedies provided by Congress.

Alternative C

To refrain from using extraordinary force

1. Jefferson Davis, who as secretary of war ordered troops to Boston at the time of the Burns crisis, had earlier, as senator from Mississippi, not only opposed Fillmore's request after the Shadrach case to expand executive power to use the militia but had also elaborated an argument suggesting a Calhoun-like preference for disunion. His mention of the marshal who failed to enforce the law and was not removed referred to the escape of William and Ellen Craft from Boston to England immediately after the Fugitive Slave Law was passed. (See pages 17, 47.)

Document†

But, sir, the case in Boston seems to be the legitimate result of an event which occurred not long since, when the officers failed to do their duty, and

†From: U.S., Congress, Senate, *Congressional Globe.* 31st Cong., 2d sess., February 18, 1851, p. 599.

the marshal who so failed was not removed. What was this but a direct encouragement to a free negro mob to set aside the law, and to oppose the officers if they attempted to execute it? I am not one of those, however anxious I may be to see this law enforced, who would advocate the use of the Army to secure its enforcement. I hold that when any State in this Union shall choose to set aside the law, it is within her sovereignty, and beyond our power. I hold that it would be a total subversion of the principles of our Government if the strong arm of the United States is to be brought to crush the known will of the people of any State in this Union. Such is my theory of this Government. If the people of Massachusetts choose to nullify the law, if they choose to obliterate the Constitution, if they choose to deny the supremacy of the laws of the United States, they will have but one step more to take, and the impulse with which they will be moving will compel them to take it; that is, to declare the authority of the United States abrogated, and the bonds of the Union to be no longer over them.

. . .

I, for one, will never give my vote to extend a single arm of the Federal power for her coercion. I trust that the history of our Government may never record such scenes as horse-guards charging upon the peasantry, or steel-clad cuirassiers turned out to ride down the ignoble rabble. The people are the sovereigns. Let them act as their wisdom and their patriotism may direct, and when they cease to have wisdom and patriotism necessary of their volition to sustain this Government, I say the Government is at an end.

2. Ohio's Salmon P. Chase, a fervent antislavery senator, opposed the reliance on troops which President Fillmore advocated (II-B-1) on practical grounds. Once again Northern extremist joined Southern in opposing a Fugitive Slave Law related measure. Thus it raises a basic interpretive question: does this phenomenon demonstrate the persistence of a large pool of shared values which should have made compromise possible? Or does it suggest, in references to revolution and disunion, a common goal of destroying a union which can contain such extremes? (See page 17.)

Document†
Well, sir, what is there strange or unusual in a rescue by force from legal custody? Such infractions of law occur not unfrequently, and in every State. Does it not seem ridiculous to fulminate proclamations and legislation against a few negroes upon an occasion like this? Surely something more than this must be designed. The proclamation and the contemplated legislation must be intended to operate upon the public sentiment of the country, to subjugate the people to the execution of the law. There can be no practical legislation except in two directions. We may provide for the erection of jails; to which no person could object, since Massachusetts has denied, as she had an undoubted right to deny, the use of her prisons for the confinement of

†From: U.S., Congress, Senate, *Congressional Globe*. 31st Cong., 2d sess., February 22, 1851, Appendix, p. 310.

persons arrested under national laws. Were there not existing provisions in the statute-book authorizing marshals, in such circumstances, to hire temporary places of confinement? We may go further, and authorize the President to call out the militia. But I ask Senators to consider where that will end. Call out the militia! March troops to Boston! What necessity is there for that? Does not every man see that the remedy is not at all adapted to the evil? You cannot prevent the occurrence of such cases as that at Boston by all the military force in the world. Occasional rescues will occur, and once rescued you cannot recapture fugitives by military force, unless you are prepared to send your troops after them to Canada. You cannot suppress the spirit of the people, unless you are prepared to establish, and the people are ready to receive, a military despotism. Governor Gage tried the experiment of a proclamation upon the people of Boston some seventy-five years ago. It resulted, not in the suppression of public sentiment, but in a revolution. The proclamation of President Fillmore will not, indeed, lead to any outbreak; but I feel quite sure that it can do no good. Sir, the ordinary authorities and processes are entirely adequate to every such case as that which has occurred; and it will be useless, and much worse than useless, in my judgment, to clothe the President with any such extraordinary powers as seem to be contemplated by the advocates of this reference. I shall not, however, object to the reference proposed. I shall say nothing against it. Let the message be referred. Let the committee act; and if Senators think fit to waste any more time of the session upon this matter, let us have their report and another debate. I desire to see, and the country will desire to see, how far it is proposed to go, not in the execution of law by its ordinary processes and officers, but in this strange attempt to suppress discussion, to prevent agitation, to restore peace, tranquility, and harmony to the country, by the employment of military force!

3. In 1854, even after troops had been used in the Burns case to enforce the law, the same questions about the role of the military to enforce the law still persisted. At that time the Democratic Richmond *Enquirer* addressed itself to the issue, judging that at best the use of force had produced only a pyrrhic victory. (See page 52.)

Document†
If the fugitive Burns had been set free by the corrupt decision of the court, or had been rescued from the custody of the law by the violence of the mob, the shock would have been felt to the remotest extremity of the Union. Such an instance of successful resistance to law and the power of the Federal Government, would have brought upon the country worse calamitous results than any foreign foe could possibly inflict. In this view the recapture of Burns is the legitimate occasion of patriotic exultation.

†From: Richmond *Enquirer*, n.d., quoted in Charleston, South Carolina, *Mercury*, June 7, 1854.

But the triumph is not complete, and we rejoice over a victory which is only not so bad as the most disastrous defeat. In so far as the interests of the South are involved, the slave might as well have been allowed to escape. With whatever success the supremacy of order was vindicated by the surrender of Burns, as regards the efficiency of the law for the recapture of fugitive slaves, the issue was determined adversely to the interests of the South. If some representative from the North were to suggest the repeal of the fugitive slave law, and were to propose instead, that the Government should compensate the owner for the loss of his property, would the South accept the offer? Certainly not; and why? Because, the proposition would substantially amount to this: that the South should be indemnified for the violation of its rights out of its own funds. Yet this compromise would be far better for the South than submission to such an execution of the law as was achieved in the case of Burns. The expense of the recapture of Burns cannot fall short of fifty thousand dollars, and as the Government assumes the responsibility of this debt, the South pays for the recovery of its stolen property in the proportion that its contribution to the federal treasury exceeds that of the North. Better would it have been for the interests of the South if the government had abstained from all endeavor to execute the law, had suffered Burns to go his way in peace, and had repaid to Mr. Suttle the full value of his slave.

Such instances of the violent repression of the popular passions by military force as we have just seen in Boston, are terrible necessities in a republican government. Despotism executes its purposes with the bayonet, but in free governments the supremacy of law is dependent on the voluntary submission of public opinion. The institutions of liberty cannot co-exist with military violence, and when a free government is driven to invoke the aid of the soldiery to carry out its laws, the day of its overthrow is not remote. Its decay has already begun, the contagion of insubordination will rapidly spread, and the exercise of military power in the repression of popular outbreaks, will be no longer a remedy in great emergencies, but an expedient of every-day and familiar resort. In such contingency, whatever may be the forms of government, a military despotism dominates, and the people are no longer free. We rejoice at the re-capture of Burns, but a few more such victories, and the South is undone.

It becomes the imperative duty of the people of the South, in view of the extraordinary and portentous circumstances of the crisis, to concert measures for their safety and for the protection of those guarantees of liberty, which northern violence exposes to such imminent hazard. We know that the public mind of the South is anxiously engaged in working out the problem of Southern duty and destiny, and that some of the most conservative and moderate men amongst us see no way of escape and no career of glory in the confederacy. But it is for the North to say if the Union shall last.

III ⸻

⸻ The Public's Alternatives

Both Congress and president realized from the start that public response was the key to the enforcement of the Fugitive Slave Law. The critical area was the North where hostility to the whole institution of slavery was widespread. How heavily would such opposition weigh when federal law and national compromise were at issue?

Alternative A

To resist enforcement of the Fugitive Slave Law

1. For Henry Bibb, himself a fugitive from Southern slavery as well as a popular antislavery lecturer, the choice was clear. Not to defy the law was to expose himself to a likely return to slavery. Significantly, by 1851, Bibb had settled in Windsor, Upper Canada, just across the border from Detroit and American law. (See page 15.)

Document†

God being my helper, though I am in favor of peace, if the human brutes under whose lashes I have smarted, come to claim me as their property, I will act as a man and a freeman, whether I am to believe the Constitution or not. If there is no alternative but to go back to slavery, or die contending for liberty, then death is far preferable. Fellow fugitives, you have but one alternative.

. . .

If a man lays hold of you, I say, resist; but if you are weak enough to suffer yourselves to be taken and carried back, then we ought to let you go. God gave the power of resistance to you, and if you do not use it in your defence, then that power should be transferred to those more worthy of having it.

2. Martin Delany was as fervent as Henry Bibb (III-A-1) in his determination to resist the law. Born free and long a resident of Pittsburgh, Pennsylvania, Delany was a physician, editor, writer, and ultimately the leading black exponent of a plan to resettle American Negroes in Africa. His address to a mass meeting in nearby Alleghany City soon after the passage of the Fugitive Slave Law was as much a challenge as it was a defence of his position. (See page 15.)

†From: "Proceedings of a Meeting of the Citizens of Boston, at Tremont Temple, Tuesday Evening, April 2d," in *Liberator*, April 12, 1850.

Document†

If any man approaches that [my] house in search of a slave,—I care not who he may be, whether constable or sheriff, magistrate or even judge of the Supreme Court—nay, let it be he who sanctioned this act to become a law, surrounded by his cabinet as his bodyguard, with the Declaration of Independence waving above his head as his banner, and the constitution of his country upon his breast as his shield,—if he crosses the threshold of my door, and I do not lay him a lifeless corpse at my feet, I hope the grave may refuse my body a resting-place, and the righteous Heaven my spirit a home.

3. Joshua R. Giddings, antislavery Congressman since 1838 from Ohio's Western Reserve, had long denied any federal power to legislate on slavery. He opposed the fugitive slave bill in the House of Representatives. When, after its passage, President Fillmore called for strict enforcement in his annual message (II-A-1), Giddings responded with a heavily emotional and moral condemnation. His speech revealed his response not only as a federal official but also as a spokesman for his constituents. (See page 14.)

Document††

The message further says, "the law is the only sure protection of the weak, and the only efficient restraint upon the strong." This, Sir, is said with direct reference to this fugitive slave law, to induce the people to execute it. It would seem that the President intended to see how far he could impose upon the intelligence of the public. Sir, what protection does this law lend to the poor, weak, oppressed, degraded slave, whose flesh has often quivered under the lash of his inhuman owner, whose youth has been spent in labor for another, whose intellect has been nearly blotted out? When he seeks an asylum in a land of freedom, this worse than barbarous law sends the officers of government to chase him down—to carry him back to chains and suffering. The people are constrained to become his pursuers. Famishing and fainting, he drags his weary limbs forward, while the whole power of the government under the President's command, the army and navy, and all the freemen of the land, are on his track, to scourge him back to bondage. And this law, the President tells us, is the only sure protection to that miserable slave. Does the President intend to insult our intelligence? Or did he mean to insert in this grave document a satire upon this barbarous enactment?

. . .

Sir, I have compared this capture of a fugitive to a common murder. In doing that I do injustice to the common murderer. To capture a slave, and send him to the South to die under a torture of five years, is far more criminal than ordinary murder, inasmuch as it adds the guilt of torture to the crime of murder.

†From: Frank Rollin [Mrs. Frances E. Rollin Whipper], *Life and Public Services of Martin R. Delany* (1883; New York: Arno Press, 1969), p. 76.

††From: "Speech on the Annual Message of the President, of December, 1850. Delivered in Committee of Whole House on the State of the Union, December 9, 1850." In Joshua R. Giddings, *Speeches in Congress* (Boston: J.P. Jewett & Co., 1853), pp. 434-35, 437.

Sir, we will not commit this crime. Let me say to the President, no power of government can compel us to involve ourselves in such guilt. No! The freemen of Ohio will never turn out to chase the panting fugitive; they will never be metamorphosed into bloodhounds, to track him to his hidingplace, and seize and drag him out, and deliver him to his tormentors. They may be shot down; the cannon and bayonet and sword may do their work upon them; they may drown the fugitives in the blood of freemen; but never will freemen stoop to the degradation of catching slaves.

4. When Unitarian clergyman and antislavery leader Theodore Parker addressed the Faneuil Hall meeting on May 26, 1854, at the time of the Burns affair, there was little doubt that he sought to sway his audience to massive resistance to the Fugitive Slave Law. Whether he was any more inflammatory than Ohio Congressman Giddings had been in the Congress in 1850 (III-A-3) may be as much a matter of the occasion as of rhetoric and substance. Did the one more than the other constitute a "clear and present danger" to the public peace? (The bracketed material in this excerpt appears in the original.) (See pages 29-32.)

Document†

FELLOW-SUBJECTS OF VIRGINIA—[Loud cries of "No," "no," and "you must take that back!"] FELLOW-CITIZENS OF BOSTON, then— ["Yes," "yes,"]—I come to condole with you at this second disgrace which is heaped on the city made illustrious by *some* of those faces that were once so familiar to our eyes. [Alluding to the portraits which *once hung* conspicuously in Faneuil Hall, but which had been removed to obscure and out-of-the-way locations.] Fellow-citizens—A deed which Virginia commands has been done in the city of John Hancock and the "brace of Adamses." It was done by a Boston hand. It was a Boston man who issued the warrant; it was a Boston Marshal who put it in execution; they are Boston men who are seeking to kidnap a citizen of Massachusetts, and send him into slavery for ever and ever. It is our fault that it is so. Eight years ago,* a merchant of Boston "kidnapped a man on the high road between Faneuil Hall and Old Quincy," at 12 o'clock,—at the noon of day,—and the next day, mechanics of this city exhibited the half-eagles they had received for their share of the spoils in enslaving a brother-man. You called a meeting in this hall. It was as crowded as it is now. I stood side by side with my friend and former neighbor, your honorable and noble Chairman tonight [George R. Russell, of

†From: Theodore Parker, *The Trial of Theodore Parker, for the "Misdemeanor" of a Speech in Faneuil Hall against Kipnapping, Before the Circuit Court of the United States, at Boston, April 3, 1855, With the Defence* (Boston: The Author, 1855), pp. 199-203. (Eds'. note: This is somewhat misleading as a title, for it is the defense Parker prepared and said he would have used had he in fact been brought to court for his role in the Burns affair. He was indicted, but the indictment was quashed.)

*The case which Parker proceeds to describe was that of Joe, a slave from New Orleans who had hidden himself aboard a Boston vessel loading at that port. When it arrived in Boston, its owners, John H. Pearson & Co., ordered Joe seized and returned to Louisiana.

West Roxbury], [Loud Cheers,] while this man who had fought for liberty in Greece, and been imprisoned for that sacred cause in the dungeons of Poland [Dr. Samuel G. Howe,] stood here and introduced to the audience that "old man eloquent," John Quincy Adams. [Loud Cheers.]

It was the last time he ever stood in Faneuil Hall. He came to defend the unalienable rights of a friendless negro slave, kidnapped in Boston. There is even no picture of John Quincy Adams tonight.

A Suffolk Grand-Jury would find no indictment against the Boston merchant for kidnapping that man. ["Shame," "shame."] If Boston had spoken then, we should not have been here to-night. We should have had no fugitive slave bill. When that bill passed, we fired a hundred guns.

Don't you remember the Union meeting held in this very hall? A man stood on this platform,—he is a Judge of the Supreme Court* now,—and he said—When a certain "Reverend gentleman"** is indicted for perjury, I should like to ask him how he will answer the charge? And when that "Reverend gentleman" rose, and asked, "Do you want an answer to your question?" Faneuil Hall cried out,—"No," "no,"—"Throw him over!" Had Faneuil Hall spoken then on the side of Truth and Freedom, we should not now be the subjects of Virginia.

Yes, we are the vassals of Virginia. She reaches her arm over the graves of our mothers, and kidnaps men in the city of the Puritans; over the graves of Samuel Adams and John Hancock. [Cries of "Shame!"] "Shame!" so I say; but who is to blame? "There is no north," said Mr. Webster. There is none. The South goes clear up to the Canada line. No, gentlemen, there is no Boston to-day. There *was* a Boston once. Now, there is a North suburb to the city of Alexandria,—that is what Boston is. [Laughter.] And you and I, fellow-subjects of the State of Virginia—[Cries of "no," "no." "Take that back again."]—I will take it back when you show me the fact is not so.—Men and brothers, (brothers, at any rate,) I am not a young man; I have heard hurrahs and cheers for liberty many times; I have not seen a great many deeds done for liberty. I ask you, are we to have deeds as well as words? ["Yes," "yes," and loud cheers.]

Now, brethren, you are brothers at any rate, whether citizens of Massachusetts or subjects of Virginia—I am a minister—and, fellow-citizens of Boston, there are two great laws in this country; one of them is the LAW OF SLAVERY; that law is declared to be a "finality." Once the Constitution was formed "to establish justice, promote tranquility, and secure the blessings of liberty to ourselves and our posterity." *Now,* the Constitution is not to secure liberty; it is to extend slavery into Nebraska. And when slavery is established there, in order to show what it is, there comes a sheriff from Alexandria, to kidnap a man in the city of Boston, and he gets a Judge of Probate, in the county of Suffolk, to issue a writ, and another Boston man to execute that writ! [Cries of "shame," "shame."]

*Benjamin R. Curtis
**This is, of course, Parker himself.

Slavery tramples on the Constitution; it treads down State Rights. Where are the Rights of Massachusetts? A fugitive slave bill Commissioner has got them all in his pocket. Where is the trial by jury? Watson Freeman has it under his Marshal's staff. Where is the great writ of personal replevin, which our fathers wrested, several hundred years ago, from the tyrants who once lorded it over Great Britain? Judge Sprague trod it under his feet! Where is the sacred right of *habeas corpus*? Deputy Marshal Riley can crush it in his hands, and Boston does not say any thing against it. Where are the laws of Massachusetts forbidding State edifices to be used as prisons for the incarceration of fugitives? They, too, are trampled underfoot. "Slavery is a finality."

These men come from Virginia, to kidnap a man here. Once, this was Boston; now, it is a Northern suburb of Alexandria. At first, when they carried a fugitive slave from Boston, they thought it was a difficult thing to do it. They had to get a Mayor to help them; they had to put chains round the Court House; they had to call out the "Sims Brigade"; it took nine days to do it. Now, they are so confident that we are subjects of Virginia, that they do not even put chains round the Court House; the police have nothing to do with it. I was told to-day that one of the officers of the city said to twenty-eight police-men, "If any man in the employment of the city meddles in this business, he will be discharged from service, without a hearing." [Great applause.] Well, gentlemen, how do you think they received that declaration? They shouted, and hurrahed, and gave three cheers. [Renewed applause.] My friend here would not have had the honor of presiding over you to-night, if application had been made a little sooner to the Mayor. Another gentleman told me that, when that man (the Mayor) was asked to preside at this meeting, he said that he regretted that all his time tonight was previously engaged. If he had known it earlier, he said, he might have been able to make arrangements to preside. When the man was arrested, he told the Marshal he regretted it, and that his sympathies were wholly with the slave. [Loud applause.] Fellow-citizens, remember that word. Hold your Mayor to it, and let it be seen that he has got a background and a foreground, which will authorize him to repeat that word in public, and act it out in Faneuil Hall. I say, so confident are the slave agents now, that they can carry off their slave in the daytime, that they do not put chains round the Court House; they have got no soldiers billeted in Faneuil Hall, as in 1851. They think they can carry this man off to-morrow morning in a cab. [Voices—"They can't do it." "Let's see them try."]

I say, there are two great laws in this country. One is the slave law. That is the law of the President of the United States; it is the law of the Commissioner; it is the law of every Marshal, and of every meanest ruffian whom the Marshal hires to execute his behests.

There is another law, which my friend, Mr. Phillips, has described in language such as I cannot equal, and therefore shall not try; I only state it in its plainest terms. It is the Law of the People when they are sure they are right and determined to go ahead. [Cheers and much confusion.]

. . .

Well, gentlemen, I say there is one law—slave law; it is everywhere. There is another law, which also is a finality; and that law, it is in your hands and your arms, and you can put it in execution, just when you see fit.

Gentlemen, I am a clergyman and a man of peace; I love peace. But there is a means, and there is an end; Liberty is the end, and sometimes peace is not the means towards it. [Applause.] Now, I want to ask you what you are going to do. [A voice—"shoot, shoot."] There are ways of managing this matter without shooting anybody. Be sure that these men who have kidnapped a man in Boston, are cowards, every mother's son of them; and if we stand up there resolutely, and declare that this man shall not go out of the city of Boston, *without shooting a gun*—[cries of "that's it," and great applause,]— then he won't go back. Now, I am going to propose that when you adjourn, it be to meet at *Court Square, to-morrow morning at nine o'clock*. As many as are in favor of that motion will raise their hands. [A large number of hands were raised, but many voices cried out, "Let's go to-night," "let's pay a visit to the slave-catchers at the Revere House," etc. "Put that question."] Do you propose to go to the Revere House to-night, then show your hands. (Some hands were held up.) It is not a vote. We shall meet at Court Square, at nine o'clock to-morrow morning.

Alternative B

To provoke disunion, civil war, and revolution

1. Abby Kelley Foster, an early abolitionist who insisted that women be full participants with men in reform, was consistently identified with the most radical fringe of antislavery. In the following excerpt from an address she gave to a convention of her colleagues, she noted the key role that resistance to enforcement of the law could play for the country as well as for individual fugitives. (See page 21.)

Document†

Mrs. Foster remarked that as far as the U[nited] S[tates] Government was concerned, it must be wholly abolished or entirely modified; speaking of the strength of the Slave Power, to-day, she granted that it looked dark; so it did in 1774, when the oppressions of the mother country were greater than at any previous time; and yet was not that very increase of oppression the cause of that resistance which overturned the oppressors' power and caused his dominion to cease? It was the *last* ounce that broke the loaded camel's back, and was not the "Fugitive Slave Law" well nigh the last ounce of aggression which the people of this land will bear? For herself, Mrs. F. added, she "saw light beyond this darkness, and thought the day of the slave's redemption was near."

†From: Abby Kelley Foster's remarks at an antislavery convention in Rochester, New York, March 13, 1851, printed in *National Anti-Slavery Standard*, April 3, 1851.

2. Scarcely a week after the abortive courthouse rescue effort and but two days after Anthony Burns was returned South, Thomas Wentworth Higginson, Worcester Unitarian minister and antislavery leader, delivered his sermon, "Massachusetts in Mourning." In danger of being indicted for murder and a variety of lesser crimes because of his central role in the rioting, Higginson was circumspect about his activities during the affray. He was not, however, about his long-range revolutionary goals or about the use to which future resistance should be put. (See pages 29-33.)

Document†

You must go back to the original Missouri Compromise, if you wish to prove that even Massachusetts punishes traitors to Freedom, by any severer penalty than a seat on her Supreme Bench.* For myself, I do not believe in these Anti-Slavery spasms of our people, for the same reason that Coleridge did not believe in ghosts, because I have seen too many of them myself. I remember when our Massachusetts delegation in Congress, signed a sort of threat that the State would withdraw from the Union if Texas came in, but it never happened. I remember the State Convention at Faneuil Hall in 1845, where the lion and the lamb lay down together, and George T. Curtis and John G. Whittier** were Secretaries; and the Convention solemnly pronounced the annexation of Texas to be "the overthrow of the Constitution, the bond of the existing Union." I remember how one speaker boasted that if Texas was voted in by joint resolution, it might be voted out by the same. But somehow, we have never mustered that amount of resolution; and when I hear of State Street petitioning for the repeal of its own Fugitive Slave Law, I remember the lesson.

For myself, I do not expect to live to see that law repealed by the votes of politicians at Washington. It can only be repealed by ourselves, upon the soil of Massachusetts. For one, I am glad to be deceived no longer. I am glad of the discovery—(no hasty thing, but gradually dawning upon me for ten years)—that I live under a despotism. I have lost the dream that ours is a land of peace and order. I have looked thoroughly through our "Fourth of July," and seen its hollowness; and I advise you to petition your City Government to revoke their appropriation for its celebration, (or give the same to the Nebraska Emigration Society,)*** and only toll the bells in all the churches, and hang the streets in black from end to end. O shall we hold such ceremonies when only some statesman is gone, and omit them over dead Freedom, whom all true statesmen only live to serve!

---

†From: Thomas Wentworth Higginson, *Massachusetts in Mourning. A Sermon, Preached in Worcester, on Sunday, June 4, 1854.* (Boston: James Munroe and Company, 1854), pp. 11-15.

*Another reference to the appointment of Benjamin R. Curtis to the Supreme Court in 1851. Both he and George T. Curtis (below) were Cotton Whigs.

**Quaker poet and abolitionist.

***Newly formed to aid free state settlers in Kansas and Nebraska.

At any rate my word of counsel to you is to learn this lesson thoroughly—*a revolution is begun!* not a Reform, but a Revolution. If you take part in politics henceforward, let it be only to bring nearer the crisis which will either save or sunder this nation—or perhaps save in sundering. I am not very hopeful, even as regards you; I know the mass of men will not make great sacrifices for Freedom, but there is more need of those who will. I have lost faith forever in numbers; I have faith only in the constancy and courage of a "forlorn hope." And for aught we know, a case may arise, this week, in Massachusetts, which may not end like the last one.

Let us speak the truth. Under the influence of Slavery, we are rapidly relapsing into that state of barbarism in which every man must rely on his own right hand for his protection. Let any man yield to his instinct of Freedom, and resist oppression, and his life is at the mercy of the first drunken officer who orders his troops to fire. For myself, existence looks worthless under such circumstances; and I can only make life worth living for, by becoming a revolutionist. The saying seems dangerous; but why not say it if one means it, as I certainly do. I respect law and order, but as the ancient Persian sage said, "*always* to obey the laws, virtue must relax much of her vigor." I see, now, that while Slavery is national, law and order must constantly be on the wrong side. I see that the case stands for me precisely as it stands for Kossuth and Mazzini,* and I must take the consequences.

. . . For one thing only I blush—that a Fugitive has ever fled from here to Canada. Let it not happen again, I charge you, if you are what you think you are. No longer conceal Fugitives and help them on, but show them and defend them. Let the Underground Railroad stop here! Say to the South that Worcester, though a part of a Republic, shall be as free as if ruled by a Queen! *Hear, O Richmond! and give ear, O Carolina! henceforth Worcester is Canada to the Slave!* And what will Worcester be to the kidnapper? I dare not tell; and I fear that the poor sinner himself, if once recognized in our streets, would scarcely get back to tell the tale.

. . .

May God help us so to redeem this oppressed and bleeding State, and to bring this people back to that simple love of Liberty, without which it must die amidst its luxuries, like the sad nations of the elder world. May we gain more iron in our souls, and have it in the right place;—have soft hearts and hard wills, not as now, soft wills and hard hearts. Then will the iron break the Northern iron and the steel no longer; and "God save the Commonwealth of Massachusetts!" will be at last a hope fulfilled.

Alternative C

To comply with a higher law

1. Charles Durkee, Free Soil representative from Wisconsin, speaking in a secular vein, based the higher law on natural rights and humanity as he sought

*Lajos Kossuth and Giuseppe Mazzini were, respectively, Hungarian and Italian leaders in the national/liberal revolutions of 1848.

repeal of the Fugitive Slave Law during congressional debates in August, 1852. He connected higher law obligations with enforcement of both Southern state law and federal law. (See page 35.)

Document†

The Federal Government was formed by those who believed in the "supremacy of God, the equality of man, and freedom of speech;" that laws were instituted to protect these rights, and that whenever they become destructive of such ends, it is the right of the people to alter or abolish them. Were the Federal Government to conspire or cooperate with a State in such tyranny, it would prove itself recreant to every rule of justice and to the great principles that called it into being. Mr. Lieber,* of South Carolina, in his Political Ethics, discusses this question in regard to the duty of obedience to unjust laws with great fullness. Here is an extract:

> We must not forget that laws may be passed in regular and lawful form, and yet be clearly against the plainest rights of the citizens, although outwardly conformable to the fundamental law. There is, however, a fundamental law superior to any fundamental charter, that is, reason, right, and nature; and that superior fundamental law of all humanity requires, in cases of high conflict, first to be obeyed. An immoral law is no law, and my yielding to it or no is a mere question of expediency, just as I may or may not yield to the demands of a robber.
> . . .

Mr. Chairman, I know it will be said that human laws, even in their greatest perfection, in many instances, work injustice, and that it is impossible for the General Government, in the administration of law, to provide for such contingencies—that the laws of Congress proceed upon general principles, and must be faithfully enforced. But I am speaking of laws upon the statute-books of some of the States, which stand out in as bold relief, and far more barbarous, than the stamp act of 1776—laws that deny a certain portion of their population the benefits of common education, by making it a penal offense to impart instruction—laws that permit one class to trespass on the rights of another, even to sensualism and prostitution, and then order the visitation of the death penalty on the innocent victim, who, in the act of self-defense, dares to strike the offender! These are the laws that Congress is called to make operative on the poor African, when he tries, through flight, to place himself in a condition of civilization and improvement! Sir, should not a Government, established to promote the general welfare, encourage such noble aspirations of the mind, rather than conspire with those who seek to suppress them, and to blot out God's image from the soul? I am bold to say, Mr. Chairman, that Congress, in enforcing the fugitive slave law, under such circumstances, is indirectly violating the letter, as well as the spirit of the Constitution, which provides, that cruel and unjust punishments shall not be

†From: U.S., Congress, House of Representatives, *Congressional Globe.* 32d Cong., 1st sess., August 6, 1852, Appendix, p. 888.

*Francis Lieber was a German-American political philosopher who taught at South Carolina College from 1835 to 1856.

inflicted, to say nothing of the fifth article of the amendments, which declares, that "no person shall be deprived of life, liberty, or property, without due process of law." I repeat, that the law of Congress requiring its officers and the people to aid in recapturing those who have become free, as did our fathers, by their own noble exertions, under the Heaven-approved love of liberty, is contrary to justice and the law of God, AND OUGHT NOT TO BE OBEYED!

2. Probably E.H. Gray's sermon to his Baptist congregation in Shelburne Falls, Massachusetts, received little attention outside the western part of his state. Rather than forming opinion, it reflected a widespread commitment not only to the obligations imposed by divine law but to the contrality of individual conscience in deciding how that law should be followed. (See page 35.)

Document†

Here, then, a most important question presents itself. Ought the Fugitive Slave Act (I will not call it a law) to be obeyed? No. Humanity says no. Conscience says no. God says no. This Slave Bill is no law; it is an abuse of human rights, an act of tyranny which would have disgraced the reign of Nero—it is a barbarous invention worthy of eternal night—it is an atrocious, villainous assault upon the rights of Freemen and Freedom—an act alike dishonorable to man and odious to God!

. . .

The Fugitive Slave Bill requires me to violate the Law of God, therefore I am absolved from it.

Any Law which requires me to disobey God, is not, and cannot be binding. This is not new or doubtful doctrine. This truth is so clear and self-evident, the marvel is, that any should fail to see and acknowledge it.

Philosophers and Moralists have fully developed it, and Jurists themselves, have frequently confessed it. Says Calvin, "If Rulers command anything against the Lord, *it ought not to have the least attention.*" Says President Edwards the younger,* "Rulers are bound to rule in the fear of God, and for the good of the people; and if they do not, then in *resisting them we are doing God service.*" Says Blackstone, the great expositor of English Law, "The Law of Nature being coeval with mankind and dictated by God himself, is of course superior in obligation to any other. It is binding over all the globe, in all countries, and at all times. *No human laws are of any validity, if contrary to this;* and such of them as are valid, derive all their force and all their authority, mediately and immediately from this original."

. . .

---

†From: E.H. Gray, *Assaults Upon Freedom! or, Kidnapping an Outrage upon Humanity and Abhorrent to God. A Discourse, Occasioned by the Rendition of Anthony Burns* (Shelburne Falls, Mass.: D.B. Gunn, 1854), pp. 12-15.

*Jonathan Edwards (1745-1801), son of the eighteenth century American Puritan theologian.

There is, therefore, a *Higher Law* to which we are held amenable, above every human law. There is a code higher and more imperative than the Constitution of America and the Declaration of Independence: it is "the CONSTITUTION OF THE UNIVERSE, and the DECLARATION OF ALMIGHTY GOD."

Away then with the dogma, that we know of no higher law as a rule for political action, than the Constitution of the United States! Against that perilous principle, by whomsoever adopted or sanctioned—against that dogma so destructive to liberty, and to all true manliness, I protest in the name of conscience and of God! there is a higher law, and you know it my hearers; a law to which all men owe obedience in all the activities of life and all the relations of society. There is a difference between right and wrong, between justice and injustice, between righteousness and wickedness; older than the Constitution,—older than all human compacts and enactments,—older and more lasting than the world itself,—it is eternal as God;—and that difference, sanctioned and guarded by the Divine Justice, is the Higher Law. In vain you may affect to be ignorant of it. Whatever you do, wherever you go, it attends you like the presence of God; every moment it hangs over you with its inexorable demands, and with the mysteriousness of its sanctions. THE HIGHER LAW! There it is! you cannot escape from it! It forces itself continually upon your intuition. That HIGHER LAW! And when you pass away from earth and time, and find yourself surrounded by the mysteries of Eternity; the Higher Law will meet you there and reckon with you.

But how is it to be known, and who is to decide when the law of God, and the law of the State, come in conflict? Shall the State decide? certainly not; for different governments, like different men, disagree as to what the Law of God teaches, and the same government often repudiates what it once demanded. As England, for instance, was formed in an age, embracing worship to the Virgin Mary, and England in the next, denounced it as idolatry, the State therefore cannot be trusted to decide whether a given law contravenes the law of God or not. Can the Church be trusted to decide that matter? Not safely. For the Church, like the State in one age, has decreed and enjoined what the Church in another age has declared impious and rejected with scorn.

Then who shall decide when the laws of God and the laws of man conflict? Each man for himself, I answer. The State cannot decide that matter, the Church cannot, but every man must decide for himself, taking God's Word for his standard.

Alternative D

To maintain law and order regardless of other issues

1. One of the most down-to-earth and practical exponents of the law and order view was Senator James Bradbury, a Democratic senator from Maine.

He had little patience with Boston radicals or others who would put themselves above the law in the name of an idealism devoid of immediate self-interest. Thus he responded to Senator Sumner's speech proposing repeal of the Fugitive Slave Law (I-E-2). (See page 35.)

Document†

But, sir, the fugitive law—the law for the rendition of fugitive slaves to their owners—is now the great bone of contention. And certain people seem horrified at the idea that they or anybody else should be required to aid in the execution of this law, and not be saved harmless for its violation. Does this law violate any of my personal rights as a citizen? Does it violate any of the personal rights of any citizen of a free State? Certainly not, except it be a personal right to resist the execution of any law we may not happen to like. That incalculable mischief, and even the destruction of everything in the form of government, would result from such a state of things, requires but few words to show.

Take the rule laid down by the opponents of this law, and make an universal application of it, and see what would be the results. The rule has been denominated the "higher law," in other words, the moral law; or, in the words of the New Testament, "As ye would that men should do unto you, do ye even so unto them." Sir, I give in to no man, in my veneration for, and attachment to, this sublime rule of right, the true concentration of all moral ethics; but I do not believe in having it strained, and twisted, and warped, to prove a favorite theory, while we leave it untouched and unused in other cases, and particularly in cases to which it is legitimately applicable. The application of this law is, as I understand it, that if I were in the condition of the fugitive slave, my wish would be that some one would aid me, and thus evade the law; that hence, it becomes my duty to do so, because I should do unto him as I should wish him to do unto me. Now, I hold that, to carry this higher law out in this manner, it would be absolutely impossible ever to inflict legal punishment for crime, even on the most atrocious wretch.

Imagine the thief, the robber, the murderer, arraigned before the judicial tribunal. The evidence is direct and positive. Not a doubt of guilt can possibly exist in the mind of any one. But, before conviction, the culprit or his counsel appeals to the court and jury under the "higher law"—the divine law—"As ye would that men should do unto you, do ye even so unto them." Think you, sir, there would be a man on the bench or in the jury-box who would not, if in the place of the criminal, wish the judge and jury to acquit him? And if the views of the higher-law advocates be correct, why not? . . .

I know, sir, that the general plea in behalf of this agitation against the fugitive slave law, and for its final repeal, is philanthropy—the professed desire to ameliorate the condition of suffering humanity; but I confess, for one, it is beyond the ken of my mental vision, to discover how the cause of

†From: U.S., Congress, Senate, *Congressional Globe*. 32d Cong., 1st sess., August 26, 1852, Appendix, p. 1123.

philanthropy and humanity is to be promoted by a process tending to produce anarchy, strife, and, perhaps, civil war and bloodshed, for the sake of aiding the escape of a few fugitives from bondage, and especially when, nine times out of ten, the condition of those fugitives, instead of being improved, is absolutely made worse. My own views of philanthropy and humanity lead me to the conclusion that, of two evils, we should choose the least; and I certainly form no just estimate of the enormous difference between the evils resulting from the return of a few fugitive slaves to their owners, and those to result to the entire people of the United States, from a course likely to annihilate the glorious fabric of the American Union. And there is still another view of this subject: I shall be borne out in the statement by every resident in a slave State, and by every man from the free States personally conversant with the subject, that, in proportion as the agitators have pushed their movements ahead, the privileges of the slaves have been curtailed; and that for all the fancied benefits secured to the few hundreds of fugitives who have escaped beyond recall, the millions remaining are made to suffer tenfold disadvantages. Whether such a result, in itself be right or wrong, matters not in the argument; the slave-owner has felt himself compelled to act on the defensive, to protect himself and his property. Admitting, then, that the hundreds of fugitives may be benefited by their change; the aid rendered them in the free States, and the settled determination to pursue that course, has indirectly inflicted a tenfold injury on the remaining millions. On which side, then, is philanthropy? I contend, then, that, even for the sake of the great body of the slaves themselves, this law ought to continue in full force, and to be rigidly executed.

2. For the conservative Whig Boston *Evening Transcript*, urging the priority of law and order was problematical because it considered the issue in moral terms and implied that a choice must be made among evils. To what extent fear and to what extent reason informed the *Transcript* editorial is an assessment each reader must make. (See page 34.)

Document†

THE LESSON OF THE DAY. The streets of our usually quiet city present a strange aspect today. Many of our citizens are called from their peaceful avocations to take up arms in defence of the laws, and to prevent anarchy and bloodshed. Patriotic and sober minded men have peculiar grievances at this time, as they have to set their lips firmly together, and "keep down some rebellious swellings of the heart." They are called upon by their fealty to Law, to suppress the inborn sentiments of their Humanity, and to keep their plighted faith with those who have just violated a solemn compact!* Many men who have never before given much attention to the subject, now ask

†From: Boston *Evening Transcript*, May 27, 1854.
*By repealing the Missouri Compromise in the passage of the Kansas-Nebraska Act.

themselves—What is our duty in this emergency? How far is the example of violating compacts to be followed?

No man, we think, familiar with public sentiment here, can deny, that the recent course pursued by the almost united South, has alienated them from the North, and created a deep seated and firmly rooted conviction, that the time has fully come, when those who remove the key stone from the arch, must not complain if they suffer damage from the fall of the ruins. They have not heeded the voice of earnest warning that went up from the wisest and best of our citizens, protesting in the name of honor and justice, against the abrogation of compromises, and affirming that a deliberate breach of the plighted faith of the nation, would tend to weaken the claims of our common country upon the confidence and affection of the people. We have done much for our engagements, our promises, our contracts. But it would seem, that not content with this, we are called upon to make new sacrifices, and to renewedly suppress the rights of conscience, of religion, and of that law, whose corner stone is justice, and whose attributes reflect the character of the Infinite.

Having thus stated the case in general terms, we would add, that to our view, there can be but one answer to the above queries. Distasteful as are the duties enjoined, and repulsive as is the task imposed, we are nevertheless required by a just regard for the cause of freedom itself, to join in no unlawful proceeding, or to countenance any measures which will not stand the test of the calmest reason, and be justified by our maturest reflection. There is a day coming after today,—in that coming day, today's heats and passions will have past, but its *records* will remain. Let every man so conduct [himself] at this time, that he may refer to that record with pleasure and honor.

A few years ago, the advocates of freedom were mobbed in our streets,* their persons were treated with indignities, and their property was destroyed. Let them see to it that, from being martyrs, they become not rioters. Folly has its martyrs as well as wisdom. Let us all trust to that benign and beneficent spirit of freedom, justice, and humanity which is now making such progress upon the earth. In this country, opinion is stronger than kings; and we may reasonably hope that our country, now the asylum for the oppressed of the Old World, will at no distant day become indeed the land of the free.

---

*Refers to antiabolitionist riots in Boston and elsewhere in Massachusetts especially in the mid-1830s.

IV

Local and State Government Alternatives

Although various Southern commentators strongly urged that Northern state and local governments should be willing to enforce the Fugitive Slave Law, their general desire to prevent federal pressures from shaping their own local and state governments' dealings with slavery kept them from pressing the issue. Furthermore the 1843 Prigg decision had left it up to each state to decide its role in enforcing the return of fugitives. Thus the alternatives in this case were fairly simple and straightforward.

Alternative A

To guarantee and protect the rights of all to due process

1. Horace Greeley, doughty reformer and editor of the New York *Tribune*, had nothing but scorn for Massachusetts Governor Emory Washburn's failure to exercise his office so as better to protect the civil rights of Anthony Burns. Clearly the editor and the governor disagreed over the latter's legal duties; and of the two Washburn was doubtless the better lawyer. After his single term as governor, he was appointed to the Harvard Law School faculty where he served as Bussey Professor until 1876. (See page 44.)

Document†

It seems to us that the great omission of duty in the Burns case, was on the part of the Governor of the Commonwealth. He stood by and saw the State authority defied and trampled under foot when the United States authorities resisted the service of the writ of personal replevin, which would have taken Burns out of the hands of the Federal authorities, and, as we understand the Massachusetts laws, would have brought the case before a jury. Here was the point where something could have been done in behalf of substantial justice. The writ of personal replevin should have been served if it had taken fifty thousand men to serve it. They would have been forthcoming if they had been wanted. But it would have taken no armed men, but only a little resolution on the part of the Governor to have vindicated the majesty of State law. But Governor Washburn disregarded the palpable duties of his

†From: New York *Daily Tribune*, June 6, 1854.

exalted station, suffered himself to be intimidated and the State to be humiliated by a paltry band of armed mercenaries of the federal power, and pusillanimously submitted to see the dignity and honor of the Commonwealth trod into the dirt.

2. After the Burns episode, Massachusetts passed its second personal liberty law in 1855, vastly enlarging the scope of the 1843 law. Adopted by the legislature in the spring, it was vetoed by Know-Nothing Governor Henry Gardner and repassed over his veto in the fall. (See page 50.)

Document†
Sect. 2. . . . Every person imprisoned or restrained of his liberty is entitled, as of right and of course, to the writ of habeas corpus. . . .

Sect. 4. The supreme judicial court, or any justice of said court before whom the writ of habeas corpus shall be made returnable, shall, on the application of any party to the proceeding, order a trial by jury as to any facts stated in the return of the officer, or as to any facts alleged, if it shall appear by the return of the officer or otherwise that the person, whose restraint or imprisonment is in question, is claimed to be held to service or labor in another state, and to have escaped from such service or labor, and may admit said person to bail in a sum not exceeding two thousand dollars. In such case, issue may be joined by a general denial of the facts alleged, the plea may be not guilty, and the jury shall have the right to return a general verdict, and the same discretion as juries have in the trial of criminal cases; and the finding of a verdict of not guilty shall be final and conclusive.

Sect. 7. If any person shall remove from the limits of this Commonwealth, or shall assist in removing therefrom, or shall come into the Commonwealth with the intention of removing or of assisting in the removing therefrom, or shall procure or assist in procuring to be so removed, any person, being in the peace thereof, who is not "held to service or labor" by the "party" making "claim," or who has not "escaped" from the "party" making "claim," or whose "service or labor" is not "due" to the "party" making "claim," within the meaning of those words in the constitution of the United States, on the pretence that such person is so held or has so escaped, or that his "service or labor" is so "due," or with the intent to subject him to such "service or labor," he shall be punished by a fine not less than one thousand nor more than five thousand dollars, and by imprisonment in the state prison not less than one nor more than five years.

Sect. 9. No person, while holding any office of honor, trust, or emolument under the laws of this Commonwealth, shall, in any capacity, issue any warrant or other process, or grant any certificate, under or by virtue of an act of Congress, approved the twelfth day of February, in the year one thousand seven hundred and ninety-three, entitled "an act respecting fugitives from justice and persons escaping from the service of their masters," or under or by

†From: *Supplement to the Revised Statutes; being the General Laws of the Commonwealth of Massachusetts. Session 1855. Prepared and Edited by Horace Gray, jr.* (Boston: Henry W. Dutton, 1855), chap. 489, pp. 278-82.

virtue of an act of Congress approved the eighteenth day of September, in the year one thousand eight hundred and fifty, entitled "an act to amend, and supplementary to, 'an act respecting fugitives from justice and persons escaping from the service of their masters,' " or shall, in any capacity serve any such warrant or other process.

Sect. 13. No person, who holds any office under the laws of the United States, which qualifies him to issue any warrant or other process, or to grant any certificate under the acts of Congress named in the ninth section of this act, or to serve the same, shall at the same time hold any office of honor, trust or emolument under the laws of this Commonwealth.

Sect. 16. The volunteer militia of this Commonwealth shall not act in any manner in the seizure, detention or rendition of any person for the reason that he is claimed or adjudged to be a fugitive from service or labor. Any member of the same who shall offend against the provisions of this section shall be punished by fine not less than one thousand, and not exceeding two thousand dollars, and by imprisonment in the state prison for not less than one, nor more than two years.

Sect. 17. The governor, by and with the advice and consent of the council, shall appoint in every county one or more commissioners, learned in the law, whose duty it shall be, in their respective counties, when any person in this State is arrested or seized, or in danger of being arrested or seized, as a fugitive from service or labor, on being informed thereof, diligently and faithfully to use all lawful means to protect, defend and secure to such alleged fugitive a fair and impartial trial by jury, and the benefits of the provisions of this act; and any attorney whose services are desired by the alleged fugitive may also act as counsel in the case.

Alternative B

To maintain law and order in crises created by enforcement of the federal Fugitive Slave Law

1. United States Marshal Watson Freeman was intent on getting the maximum aid from Boston Mayor J.V.C. Smith during the Burns crisis. The reader must assess how well, given the full circumstances of the case up until two days before Burns was put aboard the revenue cutter *Morris*, Freeman's assurance that he sought no aid in enforcing the "fugitive law" fit with his request that Boston be put under martial law. (See pages 44-45, 47-50.)

Document†

From the indications of an armed resistance to the laws, and the assurances of the military officers on duty, it is manifest that the force now

†From: Watson Freeman to J.V.C. Smith, May 30, 1854; in *William H. Ela v. J.V.C. Smith and als. Heard in Norfolk Co. Supreme Judicial Court. Feb. Term 1855* (Boston, 1855).

under the orders of Major Genl. Edmands is not sufficient to preserve the peace of the City. The Marshal has at his disposal, by order of the President of the United States, all the U.S. troops, as an armed posse comitatus, which can at present be drawn to this point. He does not ask any aid to execute the *fugitive law* as such. Nothing is required but the preservation of the peace of the city, and the suppression of organized rebellion.

To effect this, we respectfully submit an opinion, that, if bloodshed is to be prevented in the public streets, there must be such a demonstration of a military force as will overawe attack, and avoid an inevitable conflict between the armed posse of the Marshal and the rioters, and earnestly request you, under the views which Major Genl. Edmands has communicated, or will communicate to you, if desired, that you will exercise the powers the law has confided to you, to place under his command such a body of the Volunteer Militia as will ensure the peace of the city without a conflict.

From the opinion of the military gentlemen with whom we have conferred, and the indications from all other sources of information within our reach, we beg leave to express the opinion that the entire command of General Edmands within the city will be requisite. We have no express authority to pledge the General Government to that effect, but we believe that the expenses incurred by the necessity of such a military force will be met by the President.

2. Ebenezer Rockwood Hoar, who subsequently served on the Supreme Court of Massachusetts, was an attorney general of the United States, and who was turned down for a federal Supreme Court judgeship only because he opposed using federal judgeships as patronage plums, appeared before the Boston Municipal Grand Jury in 1854 to argue the illegality of Mayor Smith's actions during the Burns crisis. His argument centered on the implications which prior restraint had for civil liberties. (See pages 47-49.)

Document†

There is no law in this Commonwealth by which any district, or part of a city or town, can be put into the possession of a military force in time of peace, with power to obstruct the ordinary and reasonable use of the public ways, and to prevent peaceable citizens from transacting their lawful business—merely on account of an *anticipated* riot.

The fact that a riot has previously taken place, unless it be continuous and existing, will not alter the rule of law. And if it shall be made to appear to you that a military force has been so employed within the County of Suffolk,* and any man has been assaulted or injured thereby, or forcibly prevented from enjoying his ordinary rights as a citizen, without other justification under the law, every soldier who may have committed any such act of violence, and every officer, military or civil, who shall have ordered,

†From: Boston Municipal Court, *Charge to the Grand Jury at the July Term of the Municipal Court in Boston, 1854,* by E.R. Hoar (Boston: Little, Brown & Co., 1854), pp. 16-17, 22.

*The county in which Boston is located.

requested, caused, or procured it to be done, is, (subject only to the qualification which I shall presently state,) to be held responsible therefor.

But it is asked whether, in a case where no man doubts that a riot or unlawful assembly is impending, the civil and military commanders are obliged to wait until irreparable mischief is done, till a prisoner is rescued, a building destroyed, or blood spilled, before they can fully interpose. A sufficient answer may perhaps be found in the statement, that they may employ all the ordinary and peaceable means of enforcing the civil authority, and may have in readiness for instant employment, any amount of military force which the exigency shall demand. Further than this the law does not go, and the magistrate or officer cannot. It may seem to many worthy and prudent men that more power should be granted; but it has not been thought necessary or expedient by the framers of our Constitution and laws. The principle of American institutions is not restraint—nor intimidation—but responsibility for acts done. In relation to freedom of speech, for example, and of the press, we do not, as in some countries it is done, establish a censorship, and determine beforehand what shall be spoken or published, but we leave men free to say or print what they please, and hold them accountable for any abuse of the liberty.

. . .

It may be said that there was a great public exigency, an imminent danger; that riot and bloodshed were prevented; that there has been no considerable destruction of property, no serious personal injury inflicted; no sacrifice of life—and that it would be harsh and unwise to subject to criminal responsibility those who have acted with general good intention. Gentlemen, this is a very superficial view of the matter. All right-minded men are opposed to lawless violence. The whole community cry out against it. But when law is disregarded by its own guardians and supporters, it is "wounded in the house of its friends," and all sentiments of reverence for law in the public mind are weakened.

The old Latin maxim tells us, oppose beginnings—"Obsta principiis." Occasions where the gravest consequences have not followed, and the strongest passions are not excited, are the best to establish principles and define duties.

And if the facts which shall be laid before you require it, I have no doubt, gentlemen, that you will be ready to show to the people of the State, that laws are not made for those only who crowd the gallery or fill the dock; that whenever the strong arm of power has been raised without justification, and any citizen has suffered in his person or property, the whole community feels the wound; and that the justice, which is no respecter of persons, will allow no military or civil title to give immunity to the transgressor.

Part three

Bibliographic Essay

The student who is interested in pursuing the nature and impact of the Fugitive Slave Law of 1850 may well wish to begin his or her investigation by becoming more familiar with the general terrain, and then proceed to examine the law and its applications. This bibliography has been organized accordingly. Most of the works cited should, with a few exceptions as noted, be largely available in most college and university libraries.

For a survey of the early 1850s, Allen Nevins, *Ordeal of the Union*, 2 vols. (New York: Charles Scribner, 1947), which views events largely from a national and Northern vantage point; and Avery O. Craven, *The Growth of Southern Nationalism, 1848-1861* (Baton Rouge: Louisiana State University Press, 1953), which views the same period from a Southern perspective, are both emininently readable and judicious. James A. Rawley, *Race & Politics. Bleeding Kansas and the Coming of the Civil War* (Philadelphia: Lippincott, 1969), is still more specifically concerned with the slavery question. For the antislavery dimension of the period and the problem, one should consult Louis Filler, *The Crusade Against Slavery 1830-1860* (New York: Harper and Brothers, 1960); and Larry Gara, *The Liberty Line: The Legend of the Underground Railroad* (Lexington: University of Kentucky Press, 1961).

The long history of fugitive slave legislation, during both the colonial and national periods, is set forth with analysis and texts of major laws in Marion Gleason McDougall, *Fugitive Slaves* (1891; New York: Bergman Publishers, 1967). For a modern and detailed history of the Fugitive Slave Law of 1850, with which the present book is most directly concerned, see Holman Hamilton's study of the entire Compromise of 1850, *Prologue to Conflict: The Crisis and Compromise of 1850* (Lexington: University of Kentucky Press, 1964). Useful also in setting the background for the political dimension of the fugitive slave law controversy are the official platforms of the major and minor political parties of the day, conveniently collected in Kirk H. Porter and Donald Bruce Johnson, *National Party Platforms, 1840-1956* (Urbana: University of Illinois Press, 1956). The story of the enforcement of the law during the 1850s is told in Stanley W. Campbell, *The Slave Catchers: Enforcement of the Fugitive Slave Law, 1850-1860* (Chapel Hill: University of North Carolina Press, 1968, 1970), which argues that, on the whole, the law was successfully enforced. To complement his study, one may find a convenient survey of counter legislation in Norman L. Rosenberg, "Personal Liberty Laws and Sectional Crisis: 1850-1861," *Civil War History* 17 (March 1971): 25-44, which contends that, although the laws had little direct effect on the national crisis, they did among other things provide a good barometer to constitutional issues. In addition to Gara's study, Benjamin Quarles, *Black Abolitionists* (New York: Oxford University Press, 1969), delineates Negro defiance of the law, and observations on the law by the contemporary black leader, Frederick Douglass, are available in *The Life and Letters of Frederick Douglass*, ed. Philip Foner. 4 vols. (New York: International Publishers, 1950-55).

Serious study of the Fugitive Slave Law and its effects soon leads to other contemporary primary sources. Debates over the fugitive slave issue continued with fair frequency throughout the thirty-first, thirty-second, and thirty-third Congresses and can be followed in the *Congressional Globe;* while the statements of policy by the Administration can be found in James D. Richardson, comp., *A Compilation of the Messages and Papers of the Presidents...*, 20 vols. (New York: Bureau of National Literature, 1897-1917). Also useful for official positions is the harder to find *Official Opinions of the Attorneys General of the United States*, particularly volume 6, edited by C.C. Andrews (Washington: Robert Farnham, 1856). For both news coverage and editorial comment about the Fugitive Slave Law and the slave cases that arose under it, the files of the New York *Daily Times* and *Daily Tribune*, both available on microfilm, are useful. Larger libraries also will have microfilm editions of various newspapers throughout the country for the period. Smaller libraries may well have local newspaper runs which may report and comment upon the various fugitive cases as they occur.

Still another approach to studying the Fugitive Slave Law is the biographies of principal makers and enforcers of the law. Among them may be noted Holman Hamilton, *Zachary Taylor: Soldier in the White House* (Indianapolis: Bobbs-Merrill, 1951); Robert J. Rayback, *Millard Fillmore: Biography of a President* (Buffalo: Buffalo Historical Society, 1959); and Roy Nichols, *Franklin Pierce: Young Hickory of the Granite Hills*, rev. ed. (Philadelphia: University of Pennsylvania Press, 1958), which treat the three presidents most closely involved in the 1850 law. There is also Claude M. Fuess, *The Life of Caleb Cushing*, 2 vols. (New York: Harcourt, Brace and Co., 1923), an old-fashioned life and letters study of Pierce's Attorney General. And, in addition, there are numerous studies of various members of Congress who were active participants in the debates over writing and then enforcing the Fugitive Slave Law of 1850. Among them are David Herbert Donald, *Charles Sumner and the Coming of the Civil War* (New York: Alfred Knopf, 1961); Robert W. Johannsen, *Stephen A. Douglas* (New York: Oxford University Press, 1973); Richard H. Sewell, *John P. Hale and the Politics of Abolition* (Cambridge: Harvard University Press, 1965); James Brewer Stewart, *Joshua R. Giddings and the Tactics of Radical Politics* (Cleveland: Press of Case Western Reserve University, 1970); Hudson Strode, *Jefferson Davis: American Patriot 1808-1861* (New York: Harcourt, Brace and Co., 1955); and Glyndon G. Van Deusen, *The Life of Henry Clay* (Boston: Little, Brown and Co., 1937), and *William Henry Seward* (New York: Oxford University Press, 1967).

Two studies shed useful light on theoretical questions. Russell Nye, *Fettered Freedom: Civil Liberties and the Slavery Controversy, 1830-1860* (East Lansing: Michigan State College Press, 1949), devotes a chapter to the "Controversy over Fugitive Slaves," emphasizing particularly the issue of civil rights. The constitutional questions involved in the fugitive slave clause of the Constitution are treated briefly in Arthur Bestor, "The American Civil War as a Constitutional Crisis," *American Historical Review* 69 (January 1964): 327-52.

Turning to the question of fugitive rescue cases themselves there are several items, both primary and secondary, which deal with one or another of them. The rescue and bloodshed at Christiana, Pennsylvania, in September 1851 are covered in W.U. Hensel, *The Christiana Riot and the Treason Trials of 1851. An Historical Sketch*, (1911; New York: Negro Universities Press, 1969); James J. Robbins, *Report of the Trial of Castner Hanway for Treason, in the Resistance of the Execution of the Fugitive Slave Law of September, 1850...*, (1852; Westport: Negro Universities Press, 1970); both of which contain much primary material such as court proceedings and newspaper accounts; and Roderick W. Nash, "William Parker and the Christiana Riot," *Journal of Negro History* 46 (January 1961): 24-31, which deals with the black leader of the rescue operation. The rendition of Thomas Sims is covered in Leonard Levy, "Sims' Case: The Fugitive Slave Law in Boston in 1851," *Journal of Negro History* 35 (January 1950): 39-74. The best description of the "Jerry" rescue of October 1851 in Syracuse is the account of one of the leading participants, Samuel Joseph May, which appears in his *Some Recollections of our Antislavery Conflict* (Boston: Fields, Osgood, & Co., 1869). Jacob R. Shipherd, comp., *History of the Oberlin-Wellington Rescue*, (1859; New York: Negro Universities Press, 1969), is concerned with the last great fugitive rescue case and contains the transcript of the relevant court proceedings.

The attempted rescue and ultimate rendition of Anthony Burns can be studied in a variety of ways. Regrettably the fullest collection of source material has not been reprinted: *The Boston Slave Riot, and Trial of Anthony Burns, Containing the Report of the Faneuil Hall Meeting, the Murder of Batchelder; Theodore Parker's Lesson for the Day; Speeches of Counsel on Both Sides, Corrected by Themselves; Verbatim Report of Judge Loring's Decision; and, a Detailed Account of the Embarkation* (Boston: Fetridge and Company, 1854). More readily available are Charles Emery Stevens, *Anthony Burns. A History,* (1856; New York: Negro Universities Press, 1969); Samuel Shapiro's survey of the trial and rendition, emphasizing the link of the case to the concurrent Kansas-Nebraska debates, "Rendition of Anthony Burns," *Journal of Negro History* 44 (January 1959): 34-51; and David R. Maginnes, "The Case of the Court House Rioters in the Rendition of the Fugitive Slave Anthony Burns, 1854," *Journal of Negro History* 56 (January 1971): 31-42, which is a detailed survey of the legal proceedings against the participants in the rioting and rescue attempt. Roger Lane, *Policing the City. Boston 1822-1885* (Cambridge: Harvard University Press, 1967); and Michael S. Hindus, "A City of Mobocrats and Tyrants: Mob Violence in Boston, 1747-1863," *Issues in Criminology* 51 (Summer 1971): 55-83 both throw light on activities of the police in the Burns affair.

Additional understanding can be gained of the Burns case by looking at studies of some of the principals involved. Thomas Wentworth Higginson, who has been well portrayed in Tilden G. Edelstein, *Strange Enthusiasm: A Life of Thomas Wentworth Higginson* (New Haven: Yale University Press, 1968), has left vivid commentary of an event in which he took a leading role in his autobiographical volume, *Cheerful Yesterdays* (Boston: Houghton Mifflin Co., 1898). Henry Steele Commager enthusiastically describes Theodore Parker's role in the Burns and other fugitive cases in *Theodore Parker, Yankee Crusader,* (1936; Boston: Beacon Press, 1960). Wendell Phillips is treated in Irving H. Bartlett, *Wendell Phillips: Brahmin Radical* (Boston: Beacon Press, 1961); and Burns's chief counsel is portrayed in Charles Francis Adams, *Richard Henry Dana: A Biography,* 2 vols. (1890; Detroit: Gale Research, 1968), a large part of which is devoted to printing Dana's diary.